Manufacturing a Tradition:
A History of Lebanon Bologna

By Chris Sholly

Volume 19   Number 3

Dedication

This book is dedicated to my parents:
George A. and Anna T. Sholly

The Lebanon County Historical Society gratefully acknowledges Chris Sholly for providing this manuscript for our 2008 annual publication, to Art Communication Systems, Harrisburg, PA for their donation of layout services and to Craig H. Seltzer, President of the Palmyra Bologna Company, for his generous monetary donation towards the cost of publication.

On the Front Cover: Florence Starr Taylor (1904–1991), a native of Lancaster County, Pennsylvania, created "Food for Millions" depicting the manufacture of Lebanon bologna for the Lebanon Steel Foundry, Lebanon Pennsylvania in 1945. Ms. Taylor, after attending the Stevens (Girls) High School, went on to attend the Pennsylvania Museum School of Industrial Art on a full scholarship from 1921 to 1925. In 1926, she was invited to study at Louis Comfort Tiffany's Oyster Bay Estate. Taylor went on to careers at the Lancaster Newspapers and local PBS station WITF in 1964. She was active in many organizations as a dedicated volunteer. She passed away at the age of 86.

Table of Contents

Acknowledgements

Many people have helped me to write this book. It is based on a thesis I wrote to complete my master's degree in American Studies at Pennsylvania State University at Harrisburg in May 2007, and I would like to recognize the contributions of the people who helped me complete my master's thesis as well as those who worked with me on the publication of this book. My adviser at Penn State Harrisburg, Dr. Charles J. Kupfer, and Penn State professor Dr. Simon Bronner, both of whom helped me develop the idea and encouraged me throughout the research process.

I would be remiss if I did not mention those individuals in Lebanon County who allowed me to interview them—sometimes for hours—in order to learn the history of Lebanon Bologna. These people include Mr. H. Jack Seltzer, former Pennsylvania House Representative and president of the Palmyra Bologna Company, whose father Harvey Seltzer founded the company; his son and current company President Mr. Craig Seltzer; Mr. Ron Fouche, quality assurance manager of the Palmyra Bologna Company, whose more than 50 years in the industry served as a great resource of information; Mr. Jerry Landuyt, general manager of the Daniel Weaver Company, who took the time to tell me how he started Kutztown Bologna Company, and who pointed me to other sources of information; Mr. Clair Baum, who graciously spent a Sunday afternoon talking about the history of Baum's Bologna; Mr. Roy Burkholder, who shared his family's story; Mr. Daniel Neff and Mr. Samuel Neff, both of S. Clyde Weaver in Lancaster County, both great-grandsons of Daniel Weaver, who shared stories and photos from the family albums; and Mr. Brian Weaver of Cumberland County, also a great-grandson of Daniel Weaver, who shared his family story as well; Lebanon County Judge Robert Eby, great-grandson of bologna manufacturer Robert L. Eby; and Mr. Harry Weddle Jr., who shared photos and stories about his great-great grandfather, George T. Brooks.

The volunteers and members of the Lebanon County Historical Society showed their enthusiasm and support for this project, guiding me through old documents and helping to put together this history. They are Christine Mason, the Society's librarian; Mr. Robert Heilman, who graciously shared with me information on the history of Lebanon Bologna he had collected through his own study; Mr. David Bachman, who provided family photos showing an early Lebanon Bologna manufacturer; Annette Watts, who found newspaper articles about early Lebanon Bologna makers that helped piece the puzzle together; and Mr. Donald Rhoads for his work in helping me to publish this book.

Also, I would like to thank Lebanon Daily News publisher David L. Smith, managing editor Paul Baker and city editor Karol Gress for their continued support on this project.

Last but not least, my friend Karen Davis deserves much credit for her copyediting skills on this book and for her interest in and enthusiasm for this project.

Preface

Most Lebanon County residents grew up eating bologna sandwiches for lunch or dinner. My favorite was a piece of bologna, fried, with a good brand of mustard, between two slices of bread. But it couldn't be just any bologna between those slices of bread. It had to be the local brand, Lebanon Bologna. In fact, I didn't realize until I was about 10 years old that there was any other kind of bologna. The sandwich bologna most people buy in grocery stores across the United States is something we, in Lebanon County, refer to as "minced" bologna. Sometimes you'll also hear people refer to the other type of deli bologna as "mince meat," although more commonly that term is used to mean a pie with meat and other finely ground ingredients like fruits, and rum. Compared with the tangy taste and strong aroma of Lebanon Bologna, other types of deli or luncheon meats are bland to those of us who grew up on Lebanon's flavor. This local variety of bologna is a very different deli meat, easily recognized by its dark red color and spotted texture. It is often packaged with brand names that sound Pennsylvania Dutch—Seltzer's, Daniel Weaver's, Kutztown, Little Dutch, Baum's, or Bomberger's—or that bear some Pennsylvania Dutch symbol, such as a horse and buggy or a cartoon character of an Amish man with a beard.

When I was at college, my mother would mail a care package to me occasionally, and it always included one of my favorite treats, Lebanon Bologna. When the package would arrive, the deep aroma of Lebanon Bologna would remind me of my home in the Pennsylvania Dutch countryside. In sending the bologna, my mother was not performing an unusual practice. In fact, Lebanon Countians often send Lebanon Bologna stubs or lunchmeat packages to relatives around the world. It was a particular favorite treat for soldiers who served in the armed forces from World War I until today. Not only have families and friends sent private bologna packages over the years, but—also taking advantage of the knowledge that folks who are traveling or living far away still appreciate Lebanon Bologna—some local manufacturers have expanded their market by establishing a mail-order system.

As a young child, I didn't know Lebanon Bologna came from a Pennsylvania Dutch folk tradition. In fact, it is steeped in tradition. Its origin stretches back to the early Pennsylvania German settlers. However, it is not the only food that has links to Pennsylvania Dutch culture. Foods such as scrapple, chicken pot pie, chicken corn soup, and apple dumplings are other types of regional foods. What makes Lebanon Bologna unique in comparison with these other Pennsylvania Dutch foods is that local butchers and community businessmen successfully shifted this folk ritual from farm to factory, repackaging and commercializing this homemade product into a lunchmeat with a widespread and folksy appeal. During the peak of the American Industrial Revolution, a few entrepreneurs took this food and created a demand for it within a growing urban population. This was part of a larger national trend as the meat-packing industry was consolidating into a conglomeration of companies like Swift and Armour in Chicago. These companies focused on the mass production of meat for the urban workers. Ultimately, this would help change what Americans would eat, as well as the way they would eat, in the next century. In the late 1800s and early 1900s, there were more than a dozen manufacturers of Lebanon Bologna in Lebanon County. Today, there are two manufacturing plants in the county, and these two make most of the Lebanon Bologna that is shipped around the world.

This book explores the history and the culture of Lebanon Bologna and how it became integrated into the local community. To trace the history of Lebanon Bologna, I researched historical archives at the Lebanon County Historical Society, newspaper articles dating back to the 1860s, including the <u>Lebanon Courier</u>, one of the earliest English-language newspapers in the county, and the <u>Lebanon Daily News</u>, a newspaper started in 1872. I also researched court documents, business records, and local city directories. In addition, I interviewed more than a dozen people, including local historians, owners and managers of the commercial plants that still make the product, and descendants of businessmen who started bologna plants. Few company historical records exist intact. When researching this book, I had to rely on newspaper articles or the memories of descendants and residents, many of whom were older citizens who passed along stories, some of which could not be verified. While certain important decisions by manufacturers were noted in secondary sources, some were not. In some instances, I have speculated on what I believe may have happened based on interviews with descendants and on what was happening in the meat-packing industry throughout the United States.

The commercialization of Lebanon Bologna has economic significance for the community. It created more jobs for the local work force and added to the industrial diversity of the community, and it helped cultivate a tourist industry in the 20th century. Ironically, while the commercialization of Lebanon Bologna reduced the extent to which this product remained a part of the folk life of the local people—fewer independent farmers were making the bologna and more people were buying the company-made product—the manufacturers maintained folksy symbols to represent it. Today, a few farmers and custom butchers in Lebanon County and around Central Pennsylvania still make small amounts of bologna for their own use or for individual clients, side by side with the two main companies that mass produce large quantities for the regional and national markets. Overall, Lebanon Bologna remains a product with historical, cultural, and economic significance to the community.

Seltzer's and Weaver's are two of the oldest companies that make Lebanon Bologna. The companies promote their products in a variety of ways, such as the annual Pennsylvania State Farm Show at the Farm Show Complex in Harrisburg. (Chris Sholly)

If you ask residents of Lebanon County for the name of their bologna, you're not likely to hear them sing O-S-C-A-R M-E-Y-E-R, the famous TV commercial jingle. Lebanon natives prefer their own home-grown brand spelled L-E-B-A-N-O-N B-O-L-O-G-N-A, or as you might often hear them say with a Pennsylvania Dutch accent, "Lebnun Baloney or Ba-lone-ah." Lebanon Bologna is a bit spicier than Oscar Meyer's brand; In spite of this—or maybe because of it—Lebanon's type has been, and still is, a staple in many local refrigerators. Lebanon native Genevieve Mehler remembered having the bologna for meals as a young girl in the 1930s and 1940s:

> You could fry it. It was good when it was fried. It was good stuff, no matter how you ate it. Every man who had a job in those days took bologna sandwiches to work for lunch. That was *the* staple as far as food was concerned.[1]

While it is used mostly as a lunchmeat, it also can be eaten as an hors d'oeuvre at parties and picnics. Like some other regional food products, this Central Pennsylvania food has become a cultural artifact, evolving from a traditional farm victual into a commercially produced, regionally known meat product. For the community, it has become a social symbol of its predominantly Pennsylvania German origins. There is also a sense of pride that this product carries the name of the community in which it was invented. Lebanon County's business and government leaders have capitalized on the bologna's symbolic value, using it as a way to raise funds and to bring the community together. In the 1990s, the local tourist agency, known then as the Lebanon Valley Tourist Bureau, established the Bologna Fest, a celebration of the local bologna-making industry, as a way to attract more tourists and enhance the local economy. In addition, Lebanon Bologna acts as an emblem of the community at another event. Since the late 1990s, city officials have dropped a large bologna to bring in the New Year, another celebration of this favorite local meat.

Palmyra Bologna Company President Craig Seltzer and Denise Becker, a Lebanon County Welcome Wagon representative, add Seltzer's Lebanon Bologna to a hostess basket in this 1985 photo. The company sponsored the program for many years. (Courtesy of the Lebanon Daily News)

What is Lebanon Bologna? It is a subtype of a sausage that traces its roots in America to Pennsylvania German farmers. Many of these farmers settled in what is today Central Pennsylvania, generally the rural areas of Berks, Lancaster, Lebanon, Dauphin, and York counties in the southeastern section of the state. Lebanon County is 363 square miles, and is considered a mostly rural area, with more than 200 farms. It was carved out of portions of Dauphin and Lancaster counties, and incorporated on Feb. 16, 1813.[2] Most of the first pioneers who ventured into Lebanon County came from Philadelphia. They settled in the eastern section of the county, along the Tulpehocken Stream and Quittapahilla Creek, in the early 1700s. They purchased lands for their farms from local Native American tribes.[3] Many of these early settlers were from the Palatinate on the Rhine, a region in southwestern Germany.

These settlers were knowledgeable farmers, selecting to settle in areas with plenty of limestone—good for growing crops—and well-watered with local streams like the Tulpehocken, Swatara, and Quittapahilla creeks. The first communities formed in the county were Schaefferstown in 1741, Newmanstown in 1742, and Lebanon in 1750.[4] Early accounts of the German settlers indicate they developed a greater dependence on meat in their diets than what they had been used to in their homeland. Folklorist Don Yoder attributes this increased use of meat to the strenuous workload of the German immigrants. They spent much of their time outside working in the fields and doing other farm chores that required a great deal of energy, and they ate meat at least three times a day for that energy.[5]

Pennsylvania German farmers generally raised pigs and cows, which they would slaughter between the late fall and early spring for their year-round meat needs. Butchering day was special, a time when family and neighbors gathered together to participate in the process of slaughtering the animals and preparing the meat for consumption.[6] These farmers were thrifty, too, using every part of the slaughtered animal. Sausage was made from parts of the animal that were not used for steaks or other prime "cuts." Sausage was generally made of ground pork or beef, mixed with spices.[7] This mixture was then stuffed into a pig intestine or another type of casing, such as muslin cloth, ready to preserve.[8] The farmers used various methods of preserving the meat, such as drying, salting, pickling, or smoking it, all of which would make the meat last through the winter months.[9] Some of the farmers' sausages were given as gifts at holidays and served as a way to show that the giver had skill in making and preparing the meat.[10]

Although butchering day is no longer observed as it once was, there are still many older Lebanon County residents who can recall what typically happened on that day. Mary Greiner Wheeler grew up on a farm, about half a mile south of the city of Lebanon. That 32-acre farm became part of a small residential development in which Wheeler currently lives. Her one-story home sits on the site of the old farm home, and her back yard was at one time the site of the barn. Behind her yard, there are some stones that once formed the base of the old smokehouse where the family cured bologna and other meats. She explained what happened with the bologna:

> We cooked the bologna in a big iron kettle, and we made all beef bologna. Before that my mom would get muslin and sew bags, you know, to put the bologna in. And then we had a machine. I don't know what they called that, but it was round and had a handle and you fastened the bologna on and filled them. After we filled the bologna, we put them in the back cellar on the table. We had a big broad table. ... you left them there a couple days to get cold. And then my mom would sew them by hand. Then, we would take them up and put them in the smokehouse, and you put the dry beef in the smokehouse with the sausage, with the bacon and the bologna. ... We usually butchered on the second (of) New Year's, a steer and four pigs. They smoked pretty long, I believe.[11]

Wheeler said the smokehouse had a fireplace with an iron grill over the fire. But she said the key factor for making a good Lebanon Bologna was the smoke. Loose limestone was used in the smokehouse, which had a shingle roof where the smoke could come out.

As a young boy, Myerstown resident Roy Burkholder helped with butchering on the family farm. Burkholder's father and an uncle were butchers, and Burkholder still does some butchering of his own. The front fore of the animal would be used to make the bologna.

> Well, when my dad started out butchering, we used to hang the cattle up under the fore bay [of the barn], because it had to be so cold. It was a thing that lasted all week. You'd do your fresh meat, and of course, you'd do your sausage meat. For hamburger, we had a hand-crank grinder. Cured hams and the bolognas were put in the attic. Mom made her own [muslin] bags. Those winters were very cold. Usually January and February you'd do the butchering, when all your fall work was finished.[12]

Burkholder said his father took some of the meat they made to market and would keep some for the family's own supply.

> If we butchered for other people that family would come and help. Sometimes my dad would butcher for the hide. He would cure it and sell it to the hide man. You'd cut up the cattle and make hamburger, then he'd take out the bones, made a little scrapple and pudding, and also he would render the lard and process the bologna and sausage and the hams.[13]

To give the meat a smoky flavor, Burkholder said they would rub a liquid smoke product on the meat that hung in the attic. Cows were mostly used to make bologna. But when they could, they would use a bull, he said.

> A bull has much drier, much leaner meat, and they processed much nicer. You had a better product when you finished, but sometimes it cost a little more money.[14]

Lebanon Bologna has been documented as early as the 1780s and probably was around before then, according to Pennsylvania Dutch cooking expert, historian, and author William Woys Weaver of Devon, Pa. Of course, it probably wasn't called Lebanon Bologna until the late 1800s. By then, many of the bologna manufacturers were located in Lebanon County.[15]

Historian Don Yoder has described several different types of German sausages that eighteenth century immigrants made from butchering their animals. The first is *Broodwarscht*, or bratwurst, also called "the frying sausage." It can be smoked or unsmoked, and is made of pork with salt, pepper, sage and thyme. Sometimes beef is added to the mixture. Other sausages included *blutwarscht* or blood sausage, a spiced sausage with large chunks of white fat using the blood of an animal; *harnwarscht* or brain sausage; *Weissi warscht* or white sausage, which included tallow in the mixture; and *lewwerwarscht*, liverwurst or liver sausage, which is made from the head, heart, and liver of a pig.[16]

This old-fashioned postcard shows Weaver's Lebanon Bologna hanging in a smokehouse. Notice the Pennsylvania Dutch symbols on the sides of the postcard. This is one of the many ways in which the product is used to link the community to its past.(Courtesy of the Lebanon County Historical Society)

Another common sausage was the *summerwarscht* or summer sausage. This is a mixture of beef and pork, but mostly beef.[17] It has a tangy or sour flavor. To give it a sweet taste, farmers would add honey or brown sugar to the mixture. This sausage, which is between three to four inches in diameter, is larger than other types and it varies in length. According to Yoder, the term "bologna" most likely became applied to summer sausage because of its larger size.[18] It could be smoked or pickled. Farmers also sliced it, and ate it plain or on a sandwich. Summer sausage was one of the most popular of the sausages that Pennsylvania Germans made because it was easy to make and could be preserved without refrigeration.[19] It was these characteristics of summer sausage

Henry and Edna Bicksler wait for customers behind Henry Bicksler's Smoked Meats stand in the South Eighth Street farmers market in the 1920s. The Bicksers operated a stand there until 1952. Notice the piles of Weaver's Lebanon Bologna in the display case in front of Edna Bicksler. (Courtesy of Elsie Bicksler Hower)

that made it an ideal product to commercialize. Some entrepreneurial farmers and butchers in Lebanon County decided to improve the process of making summer sausage in the late 1800s as newly developing cities increased the demand for food, particularly meat.

This summer sausage was a regular stock item at local butchers. As happens with many recipes, each family modified the sausage by adding its own ingredients. Mary Wheeler's family made an unsweetened or what Lebanon Countians call regular bologna:

> I liked bologna and dry beef. See, you could take bologna sandwiches to school, they didn't spoil. And dry beef. We called that *frizzel* dry beef, what they call creamed dry beef today. We had a furnace in the basement, a butchering furnace, two holes to put those big iron kettles in. And that's where you cooked. We had two cellars and then we'd put them in the back cellar on a big, wide butcher table. That was for cutting up the meat. You'd cut up meat to throw in the bologna, but you had to put in a little tallow, you know, fat. We didn't make sweet bologna, just regular bologna. It had a smoky taste. And it had salt, you could taste the salt.[20]

This kind of bologna was made throughout Pennsylvania Dutch Country and throughout the United States, usually where German farmers, including those who migrated from Pennsylvania, made their homes. In some places outside of Lebanon County it is still made and called by the name summer sausage. How did this summer sausage become known as Lebanon Bologna and what ingredients make it a unique product to Lebanon?

Most people, like Mary Wheeler, believe the name derives from the place where it was first commercially produced. She explained:

> Well, because it was the bologna made here that was big bologna. That's known all over. Weaver's, that was a big thing with the smokehouses. I used to go back there and you used to go to the smokehouses and ordered your bologna. I guess it got around. Just like pretzels over at Lititz, Lancaster County.[21]

Lebanon Bologna is the creation of early Pennsylvania German settlers, who used beef and developed that certain tart flavor and deep red color that distinguishes the meat from other sausages and bolognas. As time moved on, some ingenious entrepreneurs took the settlers invention and successfully mass-produced and marketed the product using its folksy appeal on a regional and national level.

Lebanon Bologna Makers Timeline

1860-1879
George T. Brooks
Jeremiah Strayer
Lorenzo Shirk

1900-1919
Harvey Seltzer
John Weaver
Seeger Brothers
Herr & Sherman
Schaeffer & Siegrist
John Steiner
Isaac Sherman
Isaac Weaver

1950-1999
Jerry Landuyt

1880-1899
Daniel Weaver
Conrad Gerhart
Robert L. Eby

1920-1949
Daniel Baum
Daniel Bomberger
E. O. Burkholder

It is difficult to determine who was the first farmer, butcher, or businessman to coin the name "Lebanon Bologna," or what specific ingredients were used to make it a unique recipe to Lebanon County, since most bologna makers kept their recipes a secret, and still do today. It was a common product made during butchering season, generally in the winter months. Many butchers made small amounts of Lebanon Bologna and sold it in their shops. Local newspapers often published short articles about an "old-fashioned" or "traditional" butchering that described the number and weight of hogs or cows that had been butchered by local farmers or butchers. Relatives, neighbors, and friends attended the butchering to help, and they received some of the meat as a gift.

As the United States began to move from an agricultural to an industrial economy, the large-scale commercialization of Lebanon County began to take place. In 1860, the U.S. Census showed the population of Lebanon was 4,449. By 1874, that figure almost doubled to 8,160. One reason for the growth in population was the influx of immigrants from Europe, who sought jobs in the factories that were springing up around the country during this period of industrialization and urbanization. This influx of workers created a demand for commercial products and foods they could afford. Lebanon Bologna was a good, inexpensive, and convenient food with a long shelf life that became popular among the workers. It made a delicious sandwich they could take in their lunch bags, and it could be used as a meal for the entire family.

It is during the late 19th century that we see some of the first newspaper articles that mention a specific type of bologna or summer sausage associated with Lebanon. Local city directories of the late 1800s identify some of the butchers and businesses that made Lebanon bologna. For instance, Boyd's Lebanon Directory of 1883-84 lists businessman Conrad Gerhart in the business index at the front of the directory under a subheading of Bologna Manufacturers or Bologna Makers.[1] There were several others listed in the directory but not under the business index. Gerhart probably paid a premium rate to advertise his business in this index. Various companies published city and county directories each year, and their styles and formats differed. Some bologna manufacturers are listed simply as butchers, while others are listed as bologna makers. There was some turnover in the bologna-making industry as some butchers or small manufacturers retired or died and new ones took their places.

By the early 1900s, there were only a few businessmen who controlled the bologna industry in Lebanon County. Their drive and determination led them to re-invent a common summer sausage with great success. Among these early pioneers in Lebanon County are George T. Brooks, Daniel Weaver, Conrad Gerhart, Robert L. Eby, and Harvey Seltzer. Of these early enterprises, only Weaver's and Seltzer's are still in business. A few bologna companies that were started in the 20th century, such as Baum's and Kutztown, also are still being made today.

This is a photo of Lebanon butcher George T. Brooks around 1868, taken by photographer John W. Graeff at his studio at 849 Cumberland St., Lebanon. Brooks was one of the earliest, if not the first, bologna manufacturers in Lebanon County. (Courtesy of Harry Weddle Jr.)

GEORGE T. BROOKS

The earliest known mention of a Lebanon County-made bologna in a local newspaper is 1872. The following news article ran in the March 21, 1872, issue of the Lebanon Courier under a single subhead "Bolognas":

> Lebanon is becoming known for its bolognas, and the demand for them in other towns and cities is exceeding the supply. Mr. Geo. T. Brooks, who occupies as butcher the old Shirk stand in Market Square, on Ninth Street, is fast immortalizing himself among epicures by his splendid achievements in this direction.[2]

A 1911 newspaper article credits Brooks as being the original commercial manufacturer of Lebanon Bologna. It is unclear exactly when he began making bologna and whether he was the first to coin the term "Lebanon Bologna." However, one of his descendants, Harry Weddle Jr., said his great-great-grandfather first started making the bologna around 1868.[3] Brooks' one-inch advertisements in the Lebanon Courier in the early 1870s list the products he sold. The word "bologna" is typed in capital letters and is the only product that is capitalized in the advertisement.[4] By comparison, a contemporary of Brooks, a butcher by the name of Jeremiah Strayer, who also ran advertisements in the same paper, did not emphasize the word in his list of products. This could suggest that Brooks sold a special or popular type of bologna. In

Brooks Bologna Company, one of the first bologna plants in the county, was located at 147-149 North 10th Street. It is shown in this photo from the Annual Lebanon County Business and Industry book published in 1918. (Lebanon County Historical Society)

a page-size advertisement in the 1887 Lebanon County city directory, Brooks' butcher shop lists bolognas as a specialty in capitalized bold type that stands out from the other kinds of meats available from his shop.[5]   However, none of these advertisements refer to the product as Lebanon Bologna. Weddle said it was known as Brooks' Lebanon Bologna in his youth, and the <u>Lebanon Daily News</u> identified the product as Brooks' Lebanon Bologna in a 1913 article.[6] It is possible that he coined the term "Lebanon Bologna," but there is no known historical record before 1913 to prove that that was the name of his product from the beginning.

Brooks was born August 1, 1843, and died January 2, 1921, at the age of 77. He spent his early career in the shoe trade with his father George. When President Abraham Lincoln called for volunteers in 1862, the 19-year-old Brooks enlisted in the Union Army at Harrisburg, serving until the war ended, when he was mustered out on July 23, 1865.[7]   After the war, he joined his brother John C. Brooks in his butchering business. An 1868-69 business directory, however, lists a George T. Brooks with Cyrus Ramsey as Ramsey & Brooks, 1003 Chestnut Street, Lebanon, butchers. This was near the Farmers Market on Ninth Street, where many butchers had stalls to sell their products. By 1872, Brooks had started his own butchering business at the old Shirk stand in Market Square (Ninth Street) and had become well-known for his bolognas.[8] His butcher shop was located at 17 South Ninth Street.

By 1883, Brooks moved his business and home, respectively, to 149 and 147 North Tenth Street, and in 1891, his home is at 155 North Tenth Street. Brooks' manufacturing facility, including his smokehouses, was located on the west end of the city. The Quittapahilla Creek and a railroad spur ran just south of the site.[9] The spur made it convenient for the operation to receive supplies, such as barrels of spices as well as meat, and made it easy to ship the product from the plant. Like many butchers and meat manufacturers of that time, Brooks purchased beef cuts from major meat packers, such as Swift & Company or Morris and Company, both of Chicago.

In January 1913, Brooks traveled to Chicago, where he spent the week as the guest of the Morris Packing Company, one of the major meat producers of that time.[10] He took a tour of the packing plant and did some sight-seeing while there. Interestingly, the

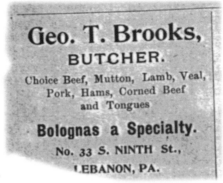

Here are two examples of early illustrations showing how butcher George T. Brooks advertised his bolognas as a specialty product. The full-page Advertisement appeared in an 1887 directory, while the small one appeared in a city directory in 1893. (Lebanon County Historical Society)

meat-packing company later proposed building its own plant in Lebanon city to make Lebanon Bologna.[11]

Although Brooks is mentioned in newspaper articles through the years, little is known about his business. However, it appears that he prospered, quickly developing a reputation for his bologna. In 1911, he added new machinery and five new smokehouses to his original thirteen to keep pace with the growing demand for his product.[12] In three weeks in 1911, Brooks made 54 tons of Lebanon Bologna, and he was credited with helping to build the nationwide reputation of the product:

> The city of Lebanon holds a nationwide celebrity for its output of palatable, wholesome, and excellent bologna. The annual production is not less than five million pounds and finds a ready sale and increasing demand in all parts of the United States. A potent factor of this well deserved renown is G.T. Brooks, the founder and present manager of the E. L. Brooks establishment, at 157 North Tenth Street, who was the original manufacturer of bologna in the metropolis of the Lebanon Valley forty-five years ago.[13]

To show the growth of Brooks' business, a 1913 news report stated that Brooks produced 1,500 pounds of Lebanon Bologna in 1893. On February 20, 1913, the amount of the product produced was 32,000 pounds, or 21 times as much as was produced 20 years earlier. After he renovated and enlarged his plant in 1913, he expected to make even more bologna.[14]

When he died, Brooks' obituary described him as an exceptionally quiet and humble man, yet a very charitable human being.[15] He left two daughters, Mrs. Lewis E. White and Miss E. Laura Brooks. His son-in-law, Lewis White probably took over the business at least for a short period. By the mid 1920s, Swift & Company bought Brooks Bologna Company. In October 1926, there were five shareholders in the company, which had

Harry L. Weddle checks the smokehouses at Brooks Bologna Company on North 10th Street in Lebanon in the 1950s. The business was sold to Swift and Company in the 1920s. Swift ran the business as a subsidiary until 1970, when it sold the operation to The Palmyra Bologna Company. (Courtesy of Harry Weddle Jr.)

Harry L. Weddle, right, mixes spices for Brooks' bologna while his father, Harry E. Weddle watches. This photo was taken between 1950 and 1951. (Courtesy of Harry Weddle Jr.)

a capital stock of $320,000. Two of the shareholders, J.H. Hall and E. W. Blatherwick, had addresses in Harrisburg, while the other three, R.H. Gifford, W.M. Sherman, and John Holmes were from Chicago.[16] Swift manufactured the bologna under the trade name of Brooks Lebanon Bologna, a division of Swift & Co. In March 1941, Brooks Bologna Company was dissolved, but the Lebanon operation continued to be managed by Brooks' descendants under Swift's name and brand until 1970, when the operation was sold to the Palmyra Bologna Company.[17] Brooks' great-great grandson Harry Weddle Jr. said the company's recipe for Lebanon Bologna was sold to Swift and has not been passed to Brooks' descendants.[18] The recipe also was not passed onto the Palmyra company, and it is believed to have been lost in the transactions.

There is one family tale regarding the Brooks company that has been passed down through generations, according to Weddle. One of the company's employees in the 1870s was Daniel Weaver, who created his own famous Lebanon Bologna recipe and built a manufacturing plant east of the city a decade later. There are, however, no company records to corroborate that story.

Brooks built his business during the early years of the Industrial Revolution. With improvements in manufacturing, refrigeration, and transportation, more butchers and businessmen tried expanding their products. By the late 1800s and early 1900s, there were a number of commercial manufacturers of Lebanon Bologna. Most likely, they were small producers. However, the history of some major manufacturers can be traced. These were men such as Conrad G. Gerhart, who was mayor of Lebanon, and wholesale grocer Robert L. Eby. Entrepreneurs like Gerhart and Eby applied the new manufacturing and transportation techniques and technologies of the Industrial Revolution. Such techniques were creating new industries as the United States began to shed its agricultural heritage. This was a time when many new commercial products were flooding the growing consumer market. And Lebanon was gaining a "world-wide" reputation for its bologna, thanks to many of its entrepreneurs.[19]

CONRAD G. GERHART

Conrad Gerhart, who was born on September 16, 1841, was described as a hardworking businessman with keen judgment and business acumen, and he was "a self-made man."[20] Gerhart's father, William, was a butcher and Conrad assisted him in the trade. Early in his career, he also worked on the Union Canal, which connected the Schuylkill Canal at Reading with the Pennsylvania Canal at Middletown, and at a cigar-making enterprise before enlisting in the Union Army.[21] When the Civil War ended, Gerhart returned to the butchering business, and in 1872, he borrowed $200 to start his own butchering venture. In the spring of 1888, Gerhart decided to specialize in making Lebanon Bologna on a large scale and set up business at 130 North Tenth Street in Lebanon.[22] This location was on the east side of the street, almost directly across from Brooks' business.

Studio portrait of Conrad Gerhart, one-time Mayor of the City of Lebanon, butcher and bologna manufacturer. (J.W. Beers & Co. Biographical Annals of Lebanon County, Pa.)

As with Brooks' operation, little is known about Gerhart's company or his product. Two articles on Gerhart in the <u>Lebanon Daily News</u> in early 1892 indicate that his business was growing. The first article stated that a Mr. P. E. Hartman of Middletown, Pennsylvania, ordered 2,500 pounds of Lebanon Bologna from Gerhart.[23] A month later, the newspaper reported that Gerhart "conducts one of the largest establishments for the manufacture of bologna sausage in the State, and the article he manufactures has gained for itself a wide reputation."[24] In this second article, the paper indicates that he started making that year's bologna in the fall. He killed seven head of cattle a week, then increased it to nine, and in some weeks, 10 cattle. In the early days of the industry, the bologna was made during the winter months and sold in the warmer months. By the end of the winter season, Gerhart was expected to have slaughtered 200 head of cattle for the purpose of making Lebanon Bologna. He employed five men to do the work for the season, and he shipped between 120 and 150 tons out of the county every year. The business brought him a "tidy fortune."[25]

An advertisement for Conrad Gerhart, bologna manufacturer, in Boyd's 1887 city directory. (Boyd's Lebanon Directory 1887)

Gerhart also was one of the organizers of the Central Market House, one of the city's first farmers' markets. In 1898, he was elected Mayor of Lebanon, and in the same period, he was elected president of the Farmers' National Bank, which he helped establish in 1892. During the last 20 years of his life—he died on Jan. 31, 1926, at the age of 85—he devoted much of his time to the bank.[26] Although he was survived by three daughters, it's not clear what happened to his bologna business. It appears, however, that he either closed the business or sold it some time between 1903 and 1907, based on listings in the city directories of that period. After 1903, Gerhart was not listed as a bologna manufacturer but rather as the president of the bank.

DANIEL WEAVER'S OLD-FASHIONED LEBANON BOLOGNA

One of the earliest bologna makers was Daniel Weaver. His company, which still exists, advertises that Weaver was the first businessman to manufacture Lebanon Bologna commercially on a large scale. Born in 1861, Weaver began farming on his own land at age 24, having acquired 70 acres in Lancaster County, according to company literature. He moved to Lebanon County and operated several farms throughout the area. He decided to move to West Myerstown, where he raised hogs, and then sold them at local farm markets. He also did some trucking, in addition to leasing a farm from the Donges Brothers.[27] About 1885, Weaver is believed to have started experimenting with a formula that would allow him to make Lebanon Bologna year-round. He started with a small amount of beef, about 200 pounds that he purchased from a Chicago

Studio portrait of Daniel Weaver. (Lebanon County Historical Society)

meat-packing house. Like many farmers of that time, he smoked it in the attic of his home, with a fire that was contained in an iron kettle. When he perfected his process, he built 26 large wooden smokehouses, and a large drying house with the capacity to cure 50 tons of the bologna.[28] Weaver added an ice house and cold storage equipment, a meat grinder, a 50-horsepower boiler, two steam engines, and a gasoline engine to his factory. He employed 15 people outside of his family to work in his plant.[29] After two years at West Myerstown, he decided he needed larger quarters for his bologna plant, so he purchased the Avondale Nursery farm, just northeast of Lebanon city, in what is today North Lebanon Township.[30] He built six houses there, which became the nucleus of the town that would later bear his name. He also had a stone-crushing business and quarry in what is today Weavertown.

Weaver was an industrious and innovative man who frequently conceived of and then pursued new business opportunities. In the early 1900s, it is believed that he established a bologna-making plant in Rochester, N.Y. A search of the Rochester city

This 1918 photo from the annual Lebanon County Business and Industry book shows the Weaver Bologna Company in Weavertown. The company is located on the same site today. (Lebanon County Historical Society)

To My Regular & New Patrons.

Having lately purchased the Goodwill and Fixtures of Schaeffer & Sechrist, Steiner & Sherman, of Lebanon, C. K. Mohler, of Lancaster, Pa., Bologna Manufacturers, and having consolidated the same, thereby greatly facilitate my increasing trade and enabling me to fill all orders promptly. I sincerely solicit the trade of the former manufacturers, and a continuance of my regular patrons.

DANIEL WEAVER,
Wholesale and Retail Dealer in and Manufacturer of

Bolognas, Prepared Ham in Brine, Tripe, Beef
and Hog Casings.

LEBANON, - - PA.

People's Telephone, No. 263. AVONDALE NURSERY 209 N. Ninth Street.

This is a copy of an early business card for Daniel Weaver. The exact date of the card is unknown, but the companies mentioned existed in the early 1900s. (Courtesy of Daniel Neff of Lancaster County)

directories between 1900 and 1910 did not turn up any meat-packing or sausage company carrying the Weaver name. It is possible that Weaver contracted with another sausage maker in the Rochester area or nearby town to produce or sell his brand of bologna. There is, however, no known historical record of such a plant.

As he was building his various businesses in the early 1900s, Weaver started yet another venture. He formed what appears to be a trade association or similar cooperative organization, which was known as the Lebanon Meat and Bologna Company. In January 1906, Pennsylvania granted a business charter to the organization located in the Mann Building in downtown Lebanon.[31] There is no record of any bologna manufacturing at this office building. The purpose of this association was to "conduct a store or stores, buying and selling freshly smoked and canned meats and large bolognas."[32]

Lebanon Meat and Bologna Company had capital of $10,000, or 10,000 shares at $1 each. The directors included most of the local bologna manufacturers. They were Daniel Weaver, George T. Brooks, Robert L. Eby, and George Seeger, the bologna makers in Lebanon, Albert Herr of Annville, Benjamin Kreider of Cleona, and Daniel K. Bomberger of Reistville, who worked for Weaver. Investors in the company included the directors and seven other shareholders, some related to the directors.[33] It is not clear why Weaver and the other businessmen decided to form this organization. One possible theory is that economic conditions at that time prompted them to form a cooperative to secure better prices for raw meat, as well as better prices for their products. Little else is known about this organization. It was eventually dissolved for unknown reasons.

Meanwhile, Weaver began to move away from bologna-making and took on new business challenges. He sold his first Lebanon Bologna plant along with his ice-making plant in Weavertown to his oldest son John S. Weaver in 1909.[34] He sold the Weavertown Water Company, which he started in 1903, and purchased what was then known as Mish's Mill, rebuilt it and enlarged a dam and millrace, and started a new venture, the Swatara Light and Power Company, selling water-generated electricity to

Employees of the Daniel Weaver Company pose outside the plant and smokehouses in 1922. The employees are from left to right: Elmer Weaver, Mary Horst, Cora Fry (wife of William), Rebecca Conrad, unknown man, James Lesher, Amanda Brandt, Sam Weaver, unknown lady, William Fry, Edward Meyer (married Daniel Weaver's daughter Caroline in 1907), Cora Weaver (wife of Sam Weaver), Edna Lentz, Miss Gettle, Nathan Weaver, Abraham Blouch, Edward Meyer (uncertain if there are two Meyers), Charlie Gettle, William Eck, unknown man. (Lebanon County Historical Society)

various communities in the county.[35] When he tried to sell electricity to residents in the city of Lebanon at a low cost, he ran into a roadblock. The Edison Electric Light Company was the main electric provider for the city. The competition that Weaver created ended in a court battle over which company could provide service to city residents. Weaver lost that battle, and was forced to sell his electric company.[36] Then, in 1918, he established a residence in Pasadena, California, and apparently intended to start a Lebanon Bologna plant there. A search of city directories there shows he lived at 2126 Foothill Boulevard in 1919-1920.[37] In the 1921 city directory, he and his wife Sarah, lived at 2625 East Foothill Boulevard and the word "Meats" follows their name in that listing. Whether or not he actually built a bologna-making plant or just a store there is not clear.

Other members of the Weaver clan also moved to California. Daniel Neff of the S. Clyde Weaver meat company in East Petersburg, Lancaster County, is Daniel Weaver's great-grandson. In 1920, when his grandmother Emma Weaver (Daniel's daughter) married S. Clyde Weaver of Lancaster County—he had the same last name but was not related to her—the couple was invited to join the family business in California. Neff said his grandparents made the trip to California, but:

> When they got there, S. Clyde became homesick, incurably so. He never got over wanting to come home. S. Clyde and Emma came back by train from the West Coast, and that was the year they started this business (S. Clyde Weaver Smoked Meats) in 1920. It appears there was a bit of a rift in the family at that point. They were not blessed for leaving the California project.[38]

By 1924, Daniel Weaver and his wife Sarah moved to 305 North Vinedo Avenue, Pasadena, and son Daniel Jr. and Rhoda (presumably Daniel Jr.'s wife) lived at the East Foothill Boulevard address. He turned over his California plant to his youngest son,

Daniel Jr.[39] What became of the business in unknown. The elder Weaver then returned to Lebanon. There is no further listing for either Weaver in Pasadena in 1926.

According to his obituary, Daniel Weaver moved to Florida, where his son Paul S. lived, in October 1925. He was 65 years old and suffered from diabetes. It was believed he moved there for health reasons.[40] He continued to dabble in business, building an apartment house there, which he later sold at a profit. He died in Sebring, Florida, on Sunday, May 23, 1926, at the age of 65. His obituary noted that: "Although he started life poor, through good management, industry and thrift, he acquired a most handsome fortune."[41]

After his father Daniel sold him the Weavertown plants, John expanded the Lebanon County business, and branched out, establishing a plant in Ciudad Juarez, Mexico, across the border from El Paso, Texas, in 1910 or 1911.[42] Mexico, particularly Ciudad Juárez, had become a major transportation hub with the growth of railroads that spread across the southern United States and Mexico.[43] The town is located in the state of Chihuahua, Mexico, and with El Paso, lies in a valley divided by the Rio Grande. Mining and the cattle industry were expanding at the beginning of the 20th century in that region, helped by the completion of the railroads. This stimulated the growth of the area, according to Mexican historian and author Oscar Martinez:

> The proximity of the border encouraged the influx of foreign capital and facilitated the penetration of northern Mexico agricultural and mining products into U.S. markets.[44]

Ciudad Juárez became the "Monte Carlo of the U.S.," according to Martinez.

Another historian, Jeffrey M. Pilcher, notes in his book, <u>The Sausage Rebellion: Public Health, Private Enterprise and Meat in Mexico City 1890-1917</u>, that Mexican businessmen and government officials were interested in importing new technology from the United States as well as Europe in the hopes of modernizing the country, thus giving it an economic boost.[45] They recruited the large meat-packing companies, like Swift, to set up modern slaughterhouses in Mexico City. Ultimately, this backfired and local butchers and citizens rebelled. It is likely that Weaver was among U.S. businessmen who found a welcoming atmosphere in Mexico, only to be caught in the rebellion backlash later. While there was no known company or historic record to explain why Weaver chose to open a plant in Mexico, it seems likely that the growth of that area offered the opportunity for him to ship more Lebanon Bologna to western states. Like many others, he also may have

John S. Weaver and his wife Lillie pose in an California orange grove about 1918. His father Daniel Weaver started a bologna business in Pasadena, Calif., where this photo is believed to have been taken. (Courtesy of The Daniel Weaver Company)

Daniel Weaver's wife, Sara, and his daughter, Emma, wife of S. Clyde Weaver of Lancaster County, take a rest along the road on a trip to California, probably around 1918. (Courtesy of Daniel Neff of Lancaster County)

Portrait of John S. Weaver, oldest son of Daniel Weaver. John took over the bologna plant in 1909. He died in a horse-and-buggy accident in August 1943. (Courtesy of Harpel's Inc.)

been attracted to the area as a place to vacation, as well as do business.

In 1910, several rival factions, including General Francisco "Pancho" Villa, rebelled against the government of Portifio Diaz. The next decade saw Villa raiding northern towns, and in August 1913, he captured Ciudad Juárez.[46]

According to H. Jack Seltzer, son of Weaver's rival, bologna manufacturer Harvey Seltzer, Weaver had a herd of cattle in Mexico at the time (as well as the bologna plant).[47] It makes sense that John Weaver would have had an intercst in this region for his cattle herd and his bologna-manufacturing plant. However, his interests in Mexico fell prey to the unrest. During at least one of the Mexican rebel raids, the bologna plant was seized by Pancho Villa for the use of his army.[48] Weaver and his main business partner at the time, Ray Sherman, were eventually forced to leave the Mexican business.[49] After the plant was seized, Weaver apparently made frequent requests to the U.S. Consul and the Mexican government to be reimbursed for his losses. The plant was estimated to be worth about $40,000. He felt the prospects of getting the plant back, or at least some compensation for it, would be better once the hostilities had ceased.[50]

Like his father Daniel before him, John also brought other members of his family into the bologna business. Lebanon resident Eleanor L. Greiner recalled her mother's tales of living in Ciudad Juárez. Her mother was Ella Weaver Bachman, who was a niece of John Weaver:

> My mother said she was about nine years old when they lived in Mexico. She said she had to cross the border [to El Paso, Texas] to go to school every day. Then, when she was about 13, they were forced to leave Mexico because of Pancho Villa.[51]

A January 1913 news article reported that Cora Weaver, her children Ella and Elmer of Juarez, Mexico, returned home after spending several weeks in Lebanon visiting

Daniel Weaver poses with an unknown young man, possibly his son Daniel Jr., and their truck. The location and the date is unknown. It is believed to have been taken in California. (Courtesy of Daniel Neff of Lancaster County)

friends and relatives. Her husband Samuel Weaver (John's brother) was apparently involved in operating the Weaver Bologna plant there.[52]

John Weaver, his family, Ray Sherman, and his other business partner had a lot of worries about the Mexican plant over the course of the decade from 1910 to 1919. In February 1912, John and Ray Sherman were concerned about the insurrection in Mexico.[53] "Several horses were stolen from them by insurrectos or rioters in the riot in Juarez several days ago," the <u>Lebanon Courier</u> reported. A year later this situation apparently had not improved. Sherman visited Lebanon, staying at the upscale Weimer Hotel. Sherman reported that the Mexican Rebellion had interfered with the operations of the plant and "caused the firm much loss." In John Weaver's obituaries in 1943, Lebanon County newspapers reported that the raid against the Mexican plant took place in 1916.[54] Various obituary notices differ in the description of the raid. One claims that Weaver was kidnapped, while another said his cattle were taken by Villa's rebels and that Weaver and Sherman were detained by Villa. After a few days, Weaver's friends, and possibly a state Senator, intervened and persuaded Villa to release him, according to the obituaries. Whether there was more than one raid on Weaver's Mexican ranch and bologna plant between 1912 and 1916 is not clear from the newspaper accounts. In a 1917 letter to his attorneys in El Paso, Texas, however, Weaver stated that he had spent "thousands of dollars and many years of worry" on the Mexican plant before Villa had forced him out. However, he still wanted to operate a plant there. He wrote:

> Our business was a good one and since I like the country I look forward to the time when we can resume operations. If these people can show us a proposition whereby we can recover our losses, we can at least listen to them. There has been considerable money spent on the plant. It is no concern of ours if General Villa chooses to put money in our property, but I wish you to make it clear that we still retain legal title to the property.[55]

In a 1955 speech to the Dauphin County Historical Society, Sara Greiner Leffler (a relative of the Weaver family) told about John Weaver's bologna experience in Mexico.

Summing up the exciting and traumatic years of the Mexican operation, Leffler said that Villa kept the plant and that Weaver's Mexican venture ultimately failed. Having suffered a large financial loss on the investment, he abandoned his Juarez site. Weaver's local partners, Ray Bicksler and Henry Bicksler, invested some money in Weaver's Lebanon operation to help him recoup some of those losses, according to Henry Bicksler's daughter, Elsie Hower.[56] The bologna company in Lebanon County that Daniel Weaver started and passed down to John stayed in the family's possession until 1981, when a group of 13 investors acquired it. The bologna operation is still located in Weavertown, although the Daniel Weaver Company and its famous Lebanon Bologna brand were again sold in February 2006 to Godshalls Quality Meats of Telford, Pennsylvania.

Portrait of Ella Weaver Bachman, daughter of Samuel and Emma Weaver, who lived in Mexico around 1911. Ella and her family were forced to leave Mexico after Weaver's Mexican plant was taken during a rebel raid by Gen. Pancho Villa sometime between 1911 and 1916. (Courtesy of Eleanor L. Greiner)

Daniel Weaver had 11 children, and most of them became involved in the bologna business at some point. One son, Jacob Weaver, should be mentioned. Jacob Weaver moved to Harrisburg, Pennsylvania, where he started a small Lebanon Bologna plant near Progress Avenue and Route 22 in the 1940s, according to his great-grandson Brian Weaver.[57] Jacob Weaver wanted to get into the business, but John and Jacob decided they didn't want to work in the same market, Brian Weaver explained. There was a big demand in the Harrisburg area, and Jacob wanted to tap into that demand, he said.

Jacob Weaver's Little Dutch brand of Lebanon Bologna was as popular as his father's. The Little Dutch brand is just slightly different than Daniel Weaver's Old-Fashioned brand. "It's just a little bit different seasonings," Brian Weaver said.

In 1957, Jacob built a larger plant at 6010 Derry Street. Until 2002, that plant was still in operation, making 10,000 pounds to 20,000 pounds of bologna a week.[58] Today, Brian Weaver makes his own Little Dutch brand of Lebanon Bologna using his great-grandfather's recipe. He finishes it in wooden smokehouses on his own farm in Mount Holly Springs, Pennsylvania. Brian Weaver has been working in the business since he was 10 years old, and he confirms that it was hard work:

> We used to bone out our own meat back in the 1950s and early 60s. you would have to put it on hooks, and it'd have to be up on the ceiling on tracks. Then you'd have to take each piece down and cut it up. It was time-consuming, and of course, a lot of heavy lifting. It was a hassle with the beef, the sides of beef weighed a ton. When you get barrels of meat, you can just use carts for that. So, we got away from that as time went on, just because of convenience.[59]

The process of making Weaver's Lebanon Bologna has changed somewhat over the past century. Some wooden smokehouses still exist at Weaver's, but they have been replaced by more modern methods of smoking the meat.

EBY BOLOGNA INC.

'A bunch of bologna women' who worked in Robert L. Eby's bologna plant pose for this circa 1916 photo. Their names are Mrs. Shirey, Demmy, Zigler, Brubaker, Hinkle, Kupehaver. (Courtesy of David Bachman)

Robert L. Eby started making bologna on a large scale in 1894 at a small, one-and-a-half story frame building, about 30 by 40 feet, located at Sixth and Oak streets in the city, with the smokehouses located at the rear of his home. The smokehouses had a capacity of 22 tons of raw bolognas, and he sold between 450 and 500 tons of bolognas annually.[60] Eby also operated a grocery business in 1909, delivering groceries by wagon initially, and then switching to the modern trucks. He employed a force of salesmen on the road to sell his bologna and other products. He also sold paper products to grocers and farmers' markets. A newspaper article credited his success to "his capacity to hustle" and his use of new technology of the day to make and sell his products. Eby was described as one of Lebanon's key businessmen.[61]

The bologna facility and smokehouses were no longer on the property at 402 South Sixth Street in 1973, according to his great-grandson Lebanon County Judge Robert J. Eby. The younger Eby purchased his great-grandfather's property that year, when he married. At the time, he did not know that the property had been in the family previously, until his father pointed it out to him. Today, apartment complexes sit on the site.[62]

Lebanon County resident and historian David Bachman lived near the Ebys. In fact, his mother, Anna Hostetter Bachman, was a young housekeeper for Robert L. Eby's family around 1916.[63] "I remember as a child walking down and visiting them, especially Lizzie, his wife," Bachman recalled.

One of the biggest dangers of bologna-making was fire. With smoldering sawdust used to smoke the bologna, fires were a common occurrence. On March 27, 1913, Mrs. William Light, who lived near the Ebys, spotted a fire at the plant around 8 p.m. Her "lusty cry of 'Fire'" aroused the neighbors, who summoned the local fire company.[64] The firemen saved the structure, as well as the homes surrounding it. The blaze, which caused about $2,000 in damage, had started in a storage area in the loft of the building. It wasn't the first fire at Eby's operation. There had been at least three fires at the plant, and there was some suspicion that the March 27th blaze was set by an arsonist.[65]

Robert L. Eby, his family and some of the people who worked in the Eby bologna plant enjoy a carefree moment in Eby's back yard, where the plant was located, around 1916. (Courtesy of David Bachman)

Eby operated his grocery and bologna businesses at Sixth and Oak streets for many years, but after the 1913 fire, he decided to move the bologna plant to another site. That may have been a result of the fire, or something more lucrative. As early as 1915, Eby had seen a business opportunity, and now he started to move on it. What he did was part of a national trend. Large companies from the Midwest were changing the paradigm for meat shipping. Eby seemed to sense these developments would be significant and enduring, and he began changing his own business model to fit the new situation.

In his book, <u>Putting Meat on the American Table: Taste, Technology, Transformation</u>, Roger Horowitz describes how the nation's large meat packers transformed the meat industry, and we can see this trend in Lebanon County.[66] By the 1880s, the large Chicago meat packers started centralizing the meat production industry by first slaughtering cattle at the stockyards, then shipping the fresh meat to the growing urban areas along the East Coast.[67] Prior to that, live cattle were shipped via railroad to local operations, where they were slaughtered and the fresh meat was then sold to the local butchers and markets. Gustavus Swift, founder of Swift & Company, found it would be less expensive and more profitable if the cattle could be slaughtered and cut in Chicago and the fresh meat shipped in a refrigerated rail car to the eastern cities.[68] One of the buyers in the early 1900s was another bologna maker, Harvey Seltzer, who was located in Palmyra. His son Jack Seltzer recalled buying meat from the Chicago packers, like Swift:

> My father bought his meat locally until he couldn't get a reliable, steady producer, so he bought carloads from Chicago packers. The shipments would take four or five days by rail in refrigerated box cars, cooled by 300-pound blocks of ice in ice bunkers at both ends of the cars. The cars would have to be re-iced every other day. The meat was packed in 400-pound barrels and we would unload them by hand.[69]

To sell his freshly cut meats, Swift created a system of branch houses that distributed his meat to the local markets in urban areas. He invested in local meat-distribution companies. Soon, other meat packers adopted his distribution system and by 1915,

In 1918, Robert L. Eby purchased this building to expand his bologna manufacturing at East Lehman and Harrison streets on the north side of the city. The photo from the annual Lebanon County Business and Industry book published in 1918. (Lebanon County Historical Society)

H. Forney Eby, son of Robert L. Eby, poses with a wheelbarrow full of Eby's Lebanon Bologna. Forney was described as the "Bologna Smoker" in the photo album from The Bachman Collection. He is standing outside the smokehouses on Oak Street in Lebanon about 1916. Notice the bologna in the casings in the wheelbarrow. Smoking is a critical step in the curing of Lebanon Bologna. (Courtesy of David Bachman)

there were branch houses in 25,000 cities across the United States.[70]

In February 1915, Eby filed an application with the Pennsylvania Department of State under the Eby Bologna Company to buy, sell, and manufacture bologna and other meat and meat products in Lebanon County. State records show there were three officers of the company: Robert L. Eby with 25 shares, his son H. Forney Eby with 25 shares, and John H. Hilbert, of 2020 South 57th St., Philadelphia, who had 50 shares. Hilbert was the treasurer. The capital stock of the company was $10,000.[71]

The following year, the Morris Packing Company of Chicago proposed to build 25 smokehouses at an undetermined site in Lebanon. The company announced that Robert L. Eby and the secretary of the Eby Bologna Company, David B. Buck, would take care of the "bologna end of the business."[72] The Morris Company had nearly 200 branches throughout the nation and Lebanon was considered a "desirable" place in which to locate a new one.

By October 1917, the local newspapers reported that Robert L. Eby needed a larger plant to meet the demands of his growing trade because his Sixth and Oak Street plant was too small. Eby purchased a meat market and defunct bologna-making operation, known as the Seeger plant, on the north side of Lebanon. He bought the property for $11,000 from Charles E. Rittle.[73] Deed records indicate that there was a house, a stable and a bologna plant on the site. Eby planned to renovate the plant, and equip it with modern machinery and electricity.[74] There was a railroad spur that ran behind the property at the time, which made it easy for Eby's products to be shipped and meat from Chicago to be delivered directly to the plant. The company apparently needed money to make the renovations to the plant and, in March 1918, a newspaper article in the <u>Lebanon Daily News</u> reported that Eby's company was increasing its capital from

$10,000 to $30,000, which was recorded with the Secretary of the Commonwealth:

> The additional stock has already been taken by the original stockholders and the money will be expended in the extension of the business. The company will shortly begin the operation of its mammoth plant at Avon, having installed modern machinery in the old Seeger plant at that place.[75]

The news article appeared two years after the Morris deal was announced, so it is likely that the Chicago company had some investment in the plant as one of its branches. In 1920, the company's name was changed from Eby Bologna Company to Lebanon Bologna and Provision Company. The board of directors and the stockholders approved the change. Vice president of the company was E. H. Risser, and David B. Buck was still secretary, according to state records.[76] The record did not include the names of other officers.

This is what the former Eby-Seeger plant looked like in 2008. The building has served many uses over the years, including an automotive business. It is the Elco Machine and Tool Company, 21 E. Lehman St. (Chris Sholly)

The new location and the switch to buying butchered meat seem to have been satisfactory, and the company grew and prospered; however, by the mid 1920s, it appears that Eby decided to get out of the bologna business. He sold the Lebanon Bologna and Provision Company about 1927 or 1928 to George A. Kessler, who lived with his family at 11 East Lehman Street in Lebanon. Meanwhile, Eby still maintained his wholesale grocery operation at 536 Oak Street. Kessler stayed in Lebanon just a few years before moving his business to Lemoyne in Cumberland County, where his descendents continue the successful business known as Kessler's Inc. Kessler's son, Robert Kessler,

---

BOLOGNA MANUFACTURER

ROBERT L. EBY
WHOLESALE GROCER
AND MANUFACTURER OF
Lebanon Bologna

PHONE, BELL 720   LEBANON, PA.

An early advertisement for Eby's Lebanon Bologna. (Ferris Bros. Lebanon City and County Directory 1887-88)

said his father made Easton bologna, which was different than Lebanon Bologna.[77] That bologna was not as popular in Lebanon, he said. The Lemoyne company today manufactures and distributes meat and other food items, including its own famous Nittany Lion Franks.

Legal issues may be one of the reasons Eby stopped making bologna. According to Lebanon County Judge Robert J. Eby, his great-grandfather had applied for a patent on his brand of bologna, but the application became entangled in the patent requirements of the day and was never granted.[78]

Robert L. Eby died in a local hospital on February 9, 1952, a few weeks after his 90th birthday. On a 1925 map of the city, the brick building in which Eby had his last bologna operation is marked simply as fabric cutting, and possibly it had become a garment factory.[79] In the past century, it also served as an automotive business. In 2008, the property was known as the Elco Machine and Tool.

PALMYRA BOLOGNA COMPANY

Harvey L. Seltzer poses at the side of his home in Palmyra, Pa. The date of the photo is unknown. Seltzer started The Palmyra Bologna Company, which makes Seltzer's Lebanon Bologna, in 1902. It is the one of two bologna companies that are still owned by the same family. (Courtesy of The Palmyra Bologna Company)

Of the early bologna-makers in Lebanon County, only one has been owned continuously by the same family: Palmyra Bologna Company. Its founder, Harvey L. Seltzer, was a farmer in the Palmyra area. His son, Jack Seltzer, said his father took home-produced meats—smoked hams, dried beef and Lebanon Bologna—from the farm to farmers' markets in Harrisburg.

A type of Lebanon Bologna was made by most farmers in the fall of the year. What my dad did was standardized the taste and quality of the product and merchandise it on a commercial basis.[80]

Like his contemporaries, Eby, Weaver, and others, Seltzer had the entrepreneurial bug. His son said Harvey Seltzer had tried to break into the shoe industry, another large industry in Lebanon County at the time:

He had wanted to manufacture shoes, but after a year at the trade, he gave it up because he couldn't stand the smell of leather.[81]

Harvey Seltzer then turned to bologna-making. According to Ronald Fouche, who is the current quality assurance manager for the company in the borough of Palmyra, Lebanon County, Seltzer "learned to make what he felt was a good Lebanon Bologna."[82] Like Weaver, Seltzer wanted to make a bologna that would keep without refrigeration,

Employees of The Palmyra Bologna Company pose outside the plant in front of a large truck with the company's logo and a Seltzer's bologna in Palmyra in this undated photo. (Courtesy of The Palmyra Bologna Company)

and he wanted to offer the product to the people who lived in nearby cities. Seltzer and Felix Burkholder founded their company in 1902. They built a plant at the rear of 230 North College Street, Palmyra, Pennsylvania. Seltzer later acquired Burkholder's shares in the company, becoming the sole proprietor. Seltzer's son Jack recalled the early days of the business:

> He talked a lot about the beginning, how he slept many a night by the smokehouse to insure proper smoking methods. In the early years, and even through my tenure, we had many failures in the creation of the proper 'bugs' to cure the bologna.[83]

In 1906, the U.S. government established the federal inspection program and Seltzer' company was one of the first to be licensed in the industry.

> We were one of the early birds, first in the Lebanon Bologna industry. It is now over 100 years that we have had continuous inspection #474. I wonder how many of the original inspected companies are still in business.[84]

In March 1912, Harvey Seltzer and his wife, Mabel (Givler), took a trip to Southern California to visit her two brothers, who were engaged in farming and growing fruits. When the couple returned, they announced they were selling their home and the bologna plant and moving to California, where Seltzer would join Mabel's brothers in business.[85] Apparently, they changed their minds. That same year, Seltzer enlarged his plant as demand for the sweet Lebanon Bologna he produced increased.[86] Jack Seltzer, today in his 80s, recalled working in the plant as a young man:

> I worked in the plant and learned how to make Lebanon Bologna. My father also had 600 acres of farm land, and I learned to farm. I, too, slept by some smokehouses and saw production failures. I learned if the product isn't 100 percent, you ditch it.[87]

Some of the Lebanon Bologna products sold by the Palmyra Bologna Company fill a display case at the company store in Palmyra. The company also sells Baum's and Bomberger products, shown in this photo. (Chris Sholly)

This is the Palmyra Bologna Company, which is located at 230 N. College St., Palmyra, Pa. (Chris Sholly)

During World War II, business for the bologna makers, including Palmyra, slowed because of the lack of fresh meat. The best meat was saved for U.S, troops, Quality Assurance Manager Fouché said.[88]

On Jan. 20, 1946, Harvey Seltzer died of pneumonia in Coral Gables, Florida, his winter home. Jack Seltzer became president of the Palmyra Bologna Company after his father's death. The younger Seltzer had a strong hand in what was done at the company. Wilbur Gibble was the general manager and secretary-treasurer of the corporation and oversaw the day-to-day operations. Jack Seltzer also ran for political office, serving seven years as a Palmyra Borough councilman, five as Council President. He was elected to the Pennsylvania State House of Representatives in 1957 and served until 1980. He served as House Speaker in 1979-1980, the year of the nuclear plant crisis at Three Mile Island in Middletown.[89] In addition to his Legislative work, the younger Seltzer spent much of his time at the bologna plant.

Today, the plant is one of the oldest, if not the oldest, business in Palmyra borough. Local historian Charles Reed gave Harvey Seltzer credit for supporting his community beyond his business. In his book, Men Who Made Palmyra: A Story Told by Dutchman, A Storyteller, Reed wrote:

> Seltzer was a visionary who developed an adaptable food product and established a company that doesn't have an equal in Palmyra's history. The community contributions of Seltzer and his family are immense because they provided for sporting, recreational, and cultural activities, such as the Seltzer Theater.[90]

Fouché joined the company in the 1950s. He has seen many changes in the industry over the years and has helped to bring about some changes. In the 1960s, he established an organization known as the Lebanon Bologna Institute.

I started that back in the 1960s. It was Baum's, Bomberger's, Weaver's and Seltzer's. We got involved in that primarily because Uncle Sam came up with the idea that all meat products were going to have to be shipped refrigerated, including canned hams. ... With that came the idea, if you had mail order, which all four of us did, your products were going to have to go under refrigeration. In those days, we basically used parcel post service. So that's how all this started. We beat the issue down.[91]

The Institute took on a number of industry issues, with its basic intent to do research into areas of concern. One of the major topics at the time centered on scientific studies that suggested nitrites used in the curing process could interact with other chemicals, producing carcinogens. Fouche recalled:

They discovered something call nitrosamines, which were secondary amines that could cause cancer. ... That's where we started. At that time all of the Lebanon Bologna makers were using nitrates, usually sodium nitrate and some were using sodium nitrite. Nitrate is NO^3, and as it breaks down it develops nitrites, that's NO^2. That went on for a good many years, and the entire meat industry got involved. We had a lot of academic and lot of research people and even the Agriculture Research Service, they got involved.[92]

The institute sent samples of its products to Lancaster Laboratories in Lancaster County for testing, Fouche said.

We tested for nitrosamines—and you could call it spending a lot of money for nothing—but that's one of the things that you do. But I think all four of us learned a tremendous amount about our products.[93]

Managers of the four companies would get together about every two weeks to discuss their concerns, and if the Lancaster lab had the results of studies on their products, they would meet with researchers at the lab, he said.[94] The theory about nitrosamines was never proven, he said.

The Institute fell by the wayside when one of its major

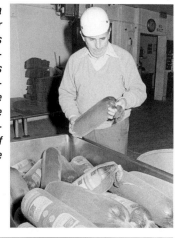

Jack Seltzer, son of Palmyra Bologna Company founder Harvey Seltzer, examines some of the company's product in this 1981 photo. This photo was taken after he retired from public office. He is a former Speaker of the Pennsylvania House of Representatives, and president of the company. (Courtesy of the Lebanon Daily News)

participants, Fred Greiner of Weaver's bologna company, died. The need for the Institute also had run its course, Fouche added.

Palmyra Bologna Company continued to expand. In 1970, the company purchased the former Brooks Lebanon Bologna plant at the rear of 155 North Tenth Street in Lebanon from Swift and Company of Illinois for $90,000. The Palmyra Bologna Company expanded its processing facilities, using the Lebanon operation for processing the raw meat before it is sent to the Palmyra smokehouses.[95]

The company was put in the national spotlight in October 1995, when it voluntarily recalled 275 tons of its bologna which may have been contaminated with Salmonella bacteria. There was no trace of the bacteria found in the meat, however.[96]

Seltzer's now also makes Bomberger's, Hatfield's, Kessler's and a few other brands, while Weaver's now makes the Kutztown brand, in addition to its own. Weaver's and Seltzer's were not the only bologna manufacturers in Lebanon County during the past 150 years; however, these two early companies and their products have survived and thrived. In addition, there were a few latecomers to the bologna industry. Among them are Bomberger's and Kutztown brands.

BAUM'S BOLOGNA COMPANY

About 1920, Daniel Baum and his cousin, Marchie Mengle, decided to go into the bologna business together on a farm north of Palmyra, Pennsylvania, according to Daniel's son, Clair Baum. "It was kind of a woodshed type deal. They bought seven cows and brought them to the farm for slaughter. Five of them had tuberculosis," Clair Baum recounted in a personal interview at his home in Elizabethtown.[97] Because buying cows had turned out badly, Daniel Baum decided to kill bulls for the bologna-making process. According to his son, that caused a rift between the two men, and Baum's father moved to his father-in-law's farm in Middletown. There, Baum developed a sweet bologna from three recipes he had learned: one from his father-in-law, one from an acquaintance, and one that he and his cousin had developed. Baum said his father delivered Baum's Lebanon Bologna by horse and wagon in the early days. In 1929, Daniel Baum moved his operation to 9427 Elizabethtown Road, Elizabethtown, where his son still lives. The buildings still exist on the property, although the processing is now done in Palmyra, Pennsylvania, by the Palmyra Bologna Company. His son recalled the early operation during an interview:

> It was a two-week process. He would slaughter a bull, debone it and put that meat into another refrigerator until it had a [certain] look. You had to look for a certain sheen, and then it was ready to make bologna. He'd make bologna Monday or Tuesday. It depended on the age of the beef. Up until World War II, my dad made both [hard and sweet] in the muslin cloth casings.[98]

The smokehouse was a key factor in the process, Baum said.

> The way my dad taught me to tend the smoke fires, we stuck our hand, our wrist into the door, and that was temperature and your forehead was your humidity. And you knew when that was right.[99]

Between 1929 and 1939, Daniel Baum built four coolers over the course of his operation. The first one held about seven bull carcasses. With the second cooler, the operation grew and the process was done every week. A third cooler was added around 1939. Each time a new cooler was added, the slaughter floor had to be moved to accommodate the changes, according to Clair Baum. In 1950, his father built what he called the "big slaughterhouse," in which he could kill 48 bulls every two weeks. Baum said his father purchased bulls from various markets, some as far away as Montana.

> If we could afford to, we'd put them on the truck or train and bring them east and slaughter them here. Dad had a carload of bulls coming from south St. Paul every two weeks. Those were all big Holstein bulls that the farmers fed out there, you know, dairy land.[100]

It was also in the 1950s that Clair and his brother, Glenn, took over the business and expanded it, adding a shipping area, more coolers, a packing and an inspection room, as well as a burning room. His brother eventually took over some farms they purchased and Clair operated the bologna plant. Under their father's operation, the company made about 8,000 pounds of Lebanon Bologna every two weeks. A the height of their operation, the brothers would make 90,000 pounds of the bologna a week.

Daniel Baum died in 1973. His son Clair ran the business until 1984. In the early 1980s, Baum said he discussed a merger with Fred Greiner, manager of the Daniel Weaver Company. However, Greiner sold the Weaver company to a group of 13 investors from Philadelphia and Reading. With new federal regulations and growing fears about nitrites—chemicals produced during the curing process which help retard bacterial growth and give the meat its coloring—business for the Baums took a downturn. Nitrites can combine with other chemicals known as amines—byproducts of proteins—to form compounds called nitrosamines, which were believed to cause cancer in laboratory animals.[101] Baum said business fell off quickly because of the nitrite scare:

> Our production dribbled from ninety-some thousand [pounds] until we got to I'd say about twenty-thousand pounds a week, and I had a lot of overhead here.[102]

The slaughtering stopped at the Elizabethtown plant in 1984, when the company went bankrupt. Baum said he contracted with the Weaver company in Lebanon County to produce Baum's Lebanon Bologna at its facilities in Lebanon County. In 2005, the Baums decided to end their association with Weaver's as the result of management changes in the company. Baum signed an agreement with the rival company, Palmyra Bologna Company, for production of Baum's bologna.[103] Palmyra Bologna Company was still making Baum's bologna in 2007.

BOMBERGER'S INC.

Employees at Bomberger's Bologna, Fox Road, Lebanon, wrap bolognas in stockinettes so the meat can be hung in the smokehouse in 1985. The firm made about 4 million pounds of Lebanon Bologna and allied products a year. It employed about 22 people at the time. The product is now made by The Palmyra Bologna Company. (Courtesy of the Lebanon Daily News)

Daniel K. Bomberger established his bologna-making company in 1920 on Fox Road near Iona. His Iona operation was located on five acres of Bomberger's farm in South Lebanon Township. In the early part of the century, Bomberger had worked for Daniel Weaver, and was a director and stockholder in the organization which Weaver started in 1906, known as the Lebanon Meat and Bologna Company. Later, Bomberger decided to go out on his own.[104] He ran his own company from 1920 until his death in 1939. Stanley L. Smith, who married Bomberger's daughter, took over the company in 1939, and in 1961, it was incorporated, with Smith as president, Carl L. Baum as vice president and general manager, and Mark O. Sheeley Jr. as secretary and treasurer.[105] In 1962, the company was purchased from Smith and owned jointly by the Palmyra Bologna Company and Wilbur Gibble.[106] By 1972, it employed 16 people, with an annual payroll of $110,000 and a gross volume of $1,400,000.[107] It made 1,500,000 pounds of bologna in 1971. By 1987, Gibble decided to retire and sold his stock in the company to the Palmyra Bologna Company. Palmyra resident Carl Baum, who was a neighbor of Jack Seltzer's, ran the plant. Baum was there from the early 1960s until he retired in 1987. The two operations were then combined. Fouĉhe said Seltzer's now makes Bomberger's sweet bologna, having purchased the recipe.

BURKHOLDER'S MEATS

Clarence Burkholder learned the butcher trade from his father E. O. Burkholder of Lancaster County in the early 20th century. In 1944, E. O. Burkholder moved his family to Lebanon County, where he plied his trade on his farm, according to his grandson, Roy Burkholder:

> We were on Kercher Avenue until approximately 1960. Then, we sold the farm and he built a shop on the site of the Kutztown Storage (659 Kutztown Road, just north of Myerstown). Then we went into retail and were also going to market. We sold all kinds of fresh meat.[108]

It wasn't until the early 1970s that the family began to produce its own brand of Lebanon Bologna, as a way to increase its meat business in the summer. The Burkholders knew a Lebanon city butcher by the name of Joe Willman. In 1973, they purchased Willman's butcher shop, then known as Joe's Bologna, Burkholder said. Willman had been in the business most of his life. His father also had been a butcher and taught his son the trade. Like many early local butchers, the Willmans had developed their own Lebanon Bologna recipe.

> Joe was interested in selling the business because of his age and his children all moved to Florida. We were also looking for something to create some more work for our workers. We'd do a lot of custom work and that is very busy in the winter. In the summertime is when your bologna and lunchmeat sells a lot more, and so we acquired the bologna business so it would create more work in the summer, more income, which it did.[109]

Clarence (left) and Ruth Burkholder pose with their son Roy Burkholder outside their bologna plant in Myerstown in April 1979. (Courtesy of Roy Burkholder)

Willman made Lebanon Bologna in the basement of his house in the city, near Maple Street. When the Burkholders bought Joe's shop, Willman was producing approximately 3,000 pounds a week, Burkholder said.

> He made it in the basement of his house, and he hung the bolognas in his smokehouse at the end of his (property) lot. He only processed it in his basement.[110]

Burkholder said the sale included Willman's recipe, as it would later when the company was sold to Kutztown Bologna Company. For six months, Willman worked for the Burkholders, teaching them how to produce his bologna. It continued to be called Joe's Bologna for the first year or so, Burkholder said. It was then changed to Burkholder's brand name.

> We made Lebanon and sweet bologna, sweet Lebanon Bologna. We probably made 80 pounds of Lebanon to 20 pounds of sweet, or 20 percent sweet. Ours was called Burkholder's Lebanon Bologna, Burkholder's Meat Products Inc. We also made some ring bologna.[111]

In those days, Burkholder said they used a natural curing process to produce their brand of bologna. The meat was aged in a cooler to start the fermentation process. It was salted, then left in the salt for 14 days. It was then processed, and smoked for approximately three to four days in the smokehouses until it was finished, he said.

> I used apple and hickory wood to hand fire it. We had two smokehouses; they each held about 6,000 pounds. They were the old wooden smokehouses. We hung the bolognas three tiers high.[112]

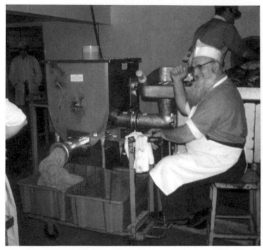

Clarence Burkholder mixes the meat for making Burk-holder's Lebanon Bologna at the plant in 1976. (Courtesy of Roy Burkholder)

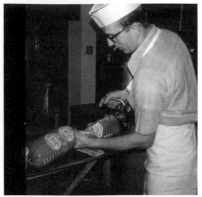

Roy Burholder stuffs the bologna into a Joe's Bologna bag. For a time after pur-chasing Joe Willman's bologna recipe, the Burkholders kept the same name for the product, Joe's Bologna. Joe and Marie Will-man taught the Burkholders how to make the bologna. (Courtesy of Roy Burkholder)

Willman put his bologna in a fibrous casing and the Burkholders used a cloth casing for their sweet brand. The sweet brands, he explained, contained much more sugar:

> You wanted it to bleed a little more so it would come out right. You had more sugar in the sweet bologna; Your meat was a lot wetter, a lot more moist, and using the cloth bag would help that to bleed more and that would help it to cure and ferment up right in the smokehouse like you needed it. With the regular (sour tasting), you didn't have that. You didn't add sugars to it.[113]

In this 1976 photo, employees at Burkholder's com-pany place Joe's Bologna into cloth or muslin bags, which were then hung in the smokehouse. (Courtesy of Roy Burkholder)

Burkholder elaborated on a number of developments in bologna making over the years. For example, when the container industry first came out with a plastic casing, Burkholder said the casing would swell and that made it difficult for bologna-manufacturers to produce a uniform product. In later years, the industry developed a fibrous casing that worked better. The first automatic stuffer Burkholder's purchased was a second-hand one, which came from the Weaver company. The stuffer was made at another local company, Kercher Machine Company in Lebanon.[114]

Although he has seen changes in the industry over the past several decades, including a trend away from processing bologna in the old-fashioned way, Burkholder continues to value some of the past practices:

> I still think the old-fashioned way, when we did the stuff naturally, was a better product. But with the costs today, you can't compete. With the starter culture, you only have to tie up one-third of your money. Before, the meat was sitting and curing, and your money was in it.[115]

Burkholder himself is no longer involved in the business, but his brother and nephew Clarence and Nelson Burkholder, respectively, still make Lebanon Bologna at their custom shop, BurPak Inc., near Myerstown. Burkholder said BurPak uses a starter culture and an automatic smokehouse, also called a smokehouse oven.

KUTZTOWN BOLOGNA COMPANY

Jerry Landuyt, now general manager at the Daniel Weaver bologna company, had been in the food business, first selling pizza and then producing bologna before he came to Weaver's. In 1979, he bought the bologna-making operation Burkholder's Meats just north of Myerstown in eastern Lebanon County, owned by Roy and Clarence Burkholder Sr.[116] In an interview, Landuyt said the Burkholders started on a farm, but they sold the farm to a company that built a small airport on the land. The Burkholders then moved their business north of town and purchased a recipe for Lebanon Bologna from Joe Willman of Lebanon, he said.

About a year after Landuyt purchased the Burkholder's bologna operation, the U.S. Post Office changed the address from Route 3, Myerstown, to Kutztown Road.[117] So, Landuyt decided to call his bologna enterprise Kutztown Bologna after the newly named road on which it was located. Landuyt started the company with a partner, who left the business after a few years. He had a vision for his new company:

> At that time, I found out that most of the stores carried only one brand of bologna. They either had Weaver, or the Burkholder name, or Seltzer's. Kuntzler was not making product at that time. The business that I was in before was pizza. You went into a store, you didn't tell them to take [a competitor's product] out, what'd you say is add this one to it and give your customers a choice. And that's how we got a foothold in the business.[118]

Landuyt saw an opportunity and took it. Although he wasn't the first to make Lebanon Bologna, Landuyt was an innovator who embraced technological changes that were then followed by other bologna makers. For example, Landuyt used a starter culture to accelerate the curing process.

Elaine Kreiser, an employee of Kutztown Bologna Company, and Jerry Landuyt, company president, inspect packages of the company's low-salt bologna products in this June 1988 photo. The product had a third less salt than Kutztown's original Lebanon Bologna. Landuyt said the company found a small market for the product, especially as consumers became more health-conscious about their eating habits. (Courtesy of the Lebanon Daily News)

A firefighter shoots water on the roof of the Kutztown Bologna Company plant in Jackson Township, Lebanon County, as employees watch after an early morning fire destroyed the business on December 5, 2000. (Courtesy of the Lebanon Daily News)

> If you go back quite a few years, you'll find that the Seltzer company never used starter culture nor did Weaver's use starter culture. And the Burkholders didn't. We found out if we used starter culture, we could make the same product all the time. And starter culture was used for Salami, and many different products like that. You actually moved the process up quite a few days. That helped the aging of the product.[119]

Kutztown Bologna Company started with approximately nine employees. As the bologna business grew, Landuyt started adding products, such as ring bologna, turkey breast, and roast beef, for example. The company started with annual sales estimated at $1,000,000 and in a matter of years, sales grew to more than $7,000,000. This figure included all of the company's products, not just Lebanon Bologna. Among the "firsts" claimed for the Kutztown brand include the first honey bologna, the first low-salt Lebanon Bologna, and the first 95 percent low-fat bologna. Landuyt credited those firsts to the company's marketing people. The company aggressively marketed its products.

> We knew we were fighting bigger companies, so we just took little niches here and little niches there. Weaver's seemed to be satisfied where it was in the market at the time, not promoting its product very much.[120]

Landuyt's success took a tragic turn when a fire destroyed the Kutztown operation in 2000. It was a tough time for Landuyt and his workers.

> I was looking for a place to rebuild or to go someplace else. Right after the fire, I was trying to find someone who could make product for us. I was able to find somebody. I knew somebody through the Pennsylvania Meat Association that I called, and they suggested the Godshalls plant in Telford (Montgomery County, Pa.). That's how I got started with them. And one of the main reasons why I didn't rebuild where I was is that there was not sewer or water out there … and to build a $4 million to $5 million plant without having water and sewer was just not the thing to do. So, I would have had to move, buy another piece of land, start all over, and frankly I had turned 60 years old and I didn't want to take that big step again and go into debt. When the Burkholders had it, it was a small plant, a custom butcher shop. We added on to it, probably four times bigger than what they had. As it turns out, that was part of my problem. It was under a whole bunch of different roofs, and when it caught on fire they couldn't get a hold of it. It was not a good day.[121]

Landuyt reached an agreement with Godshalls Quality Meats to make his Kutztown bologna at their Telford, Pa., plant for a time. Then, about three years after the fire, Landuyt, who was nearing retirement, asked the owners of the Weaver's operation if they would make Kutztown Lebanon Bologna. Landuyt worked out an agreement with Weaver's to make his brand of bologna there, eventually switching from Godshalls. Initially, Landuyt wanted to make sure his own product was being made according to his instructions, and so he oversaw the production of the product at Weaver's plant. As he worked with Weaver's management team at that time, Landuyt became more and more involved in the plant's daily operations. He watched as the company fell on hard times:

> In fact, they were going to close the doors. I offered to come in and see what I could do and the owners gave me a chance. Within a year we stopped the bleeding and started to turn it around.[122]

Godshalls then purchased Weaver's in 2006 and now owns and runs its Telford operation plus the Weaver's Lebanon County business. Godshalls has spent millions of dollars on improving the plant and have added new technology and equipment.[123]

OTHER BOLOGNA MAKERS

Several other bologna manufacturers are mentioned in Lebanon city directories or news articles but little is known about them. Still, they are worth mentioning.

Keystone Sausage Works Inc. (later Seeger Brothers) was started by brothers, George J., Edward, and later, Frederick Seeger. Initially, Keystone Sausage Works operated at 19 South Ninth Street, according to Shaffer's Directory of the City of

Lebanon, Pa. & Suburbs.[124] By 1907, the company is listed in R. L. Polk & Co.'s Lebanon Directory as Seeger Brothers, East Lehman and Harrison Streets.[125] The brothers formed a partnership in 1908 to operate a retail meat business in Lebanon.[126] They had purchased a meat market at East Lehman and Harrison streets, which had been owned by Jacob Weaver, who was a son of bologna manufacturer Daniel Weaver.

Frederick Seeger joined his brother Edward in the business after having been employed for some years by Armour and Company at Chicago.[127] An article in a Reading newspaper dated June 16, 1908, stated the following:

> Seeger Brothers have begun work on the erection of a new bologna manufacturing establishment near Avon. The plant will be located some distance west of Seeger's present extensive operation at that place and is to be in working order at an early date.[128]

The business, however, didn't last long. The last mention of the Seeger Brothers business is in Polk's 1909 directory, which lists Christian H. Seeger, one of the brothers, as the owner. He died in 1911 and in January 1912, a Lebanon County judge granted an order that allowed the sale of the entire property, including the plant, as part of the estate.[129] The property was sold at a sheriff's sale in September 1913 to the Lancaster law firm of Appel and Appel, representing parties interested in the estate, for $5,000.[130] The plant was sold to other buyers over the next several years. It continued to operate as a bologna plant. The property and plant were later purchased by Robert L. Eby.

Chris Sholly

This white garden shed was once the office of the Herr & Sherman Bologna Company in Annville. The office was purchased after the company went out of business and stands in the back yard of Annville historian Blanche Schaeffer.

Herr & Sherman was located at Railroad Street in Annville. The company was near the Pennsylvania and Reading Railroad Station. The company is listed in Lebanon city directories from about 1907 to 1909.[131] In January 1906, two articles in the <u>Annville Journal</u> mentioned the company. The first noted that the company installed a 20-horsepower engine at the plant.[132] The engine helped increase the plant's output. The second article noted that Albert Herr and Joseph G. Kelchner, both of Annville, were two of the stockholders in the Lebanon Meat and Bologna Company, which apparently was a trade association.[133]

Blanche M. Schaeffer of Annville said her great-grandfather, Harry Boltz, bought the office of the Herr & Sherman bologna company, which was a small, wood-paneled one-room building with a pot belly stove, for $50 in the 1920s. She said he moved it to his home at 50 N. King St. to house his shoe shop. The shop is still located on the Schaeffer property, but the family has used for years as a garden shed. Inside the door, letters spelling Herr & Sherman can still be seen through the white paint.[134]

Isaac Sherman, 307-309 N. Ninth St., Lebanon, is listed in Lebanon city directories 1901 and 1903 as a manufacturer of Lebanon Bologna.[135]

John Steiner, 421 Walnut St., Lebanon, is listed as a bologna manufacturer in the city directory in 1901.[136]

Schaeffer & Siegrist was located at 336 S. Sixth St., Lebanon. The company is listed in the city directory in 1901.[137] Daniel Weaver purchased the "Goodwill and Fixtures" of this company, as well as Steiner's and Sherman's, and C.K. Mohler of Lancaster County, then consolidated them under his own business at Avondale Nursery sometime in the early 1900s. [138]

Jeremiah Strayer was one of the early manufacturer's of Lebanon Bologna, a contemporary of George T. Brooks, in fact. The Lebanon Courier in its edition of February 22, 1872, published a short paragraph about Strayer, which read, "Lebanon bolognas are gaining a wide reputation. Mr. Jeremiah Strayer, last week, sold 5, 000 pounds of the article to Pottsville." [139] Strayer is listed in the city directories as a butcher until 1915. Little else is known about his operation.

Isaac Weaver had a bologna business located in Avondale about 1901 to 1903. It's unknown if he was related to Daniel Weaver. [140]

Lebanon Bologna comes in a variety of sizes, flavors, and brands. Godshalls, the current owner of Weaver's original plant, produces a regular and a sweet variety of the bologna under the Daniel Weaver brand, while the Palmyra Bologna Company produces a sweet variety of its own, as well as Baum's and Bomberger's brands. As consumers have become more health conscious, the companies have added low-sodium and low-fat varieties to their original bolognas, as well as double-smoked, leaner beef cuts and thin-slice varieties. Each company boasts its own "secret" recipe, and these recipes vary primarily in the mixture of spices, brown sugar, or honey used in the process.

Each one of the 10 smokehouses at the Palmyra Bologna Company can hold up to 16,000 pounds of product. (Chris Sholly)

Lebanon Bologna is made with 90 percent all lean beef under the United States Department of Agriculture regulations. No binders or extenders may be used. With the exception of modern technology, the actual process of making Lebanon Bologna is similar to the way the early settlers made it. Manufacturers start with fresh meat, which is coarsely ground in large containers. The spices are then added to the meat, and it is ground again. The ground meat is salted, and then allowed to age at a temperature of about 5 degrees Celsius (41 degrees Fahrenheit) for up to 10 days. This aging allows lactic acid bacteria and micrococci to develop.[1] Lactic acids bacteria help give the bologna its taste and dark red color, while the salt inhibits bacterial growth.[2] The meat is then stuffed into a casing—in the early days, pig intestines were used while in current commercial operations plastic or cellulose bags are generally used—then clipped tightly. The meat in the casing is hung in a wooden or stainless steel smokehouse from 36 to 60 hours to finish the product. In a wooden smokehouse, fires are contained in a pit, which has a metal grill over the top of it. On top of the grill workers place sawdust that is sprayed with water. This allows the smoke to penetrate the meat and the moisture to escape. After it is smoked, the bologna is cooled down before it is ready for consumption or to be shipped to the retail stores. Some companies, such as Godshalls, use a starter culture to accelerate the fermentation process.

Roy Burkholder said the Burkholder's brand of bologna was processed using natural curing rather than the starter culture.

> We cured the meat in the cooler, which aged it and caused the fermentation. We salted it down, and left it in the salt for 14 days to ferment it, and then we processed it, and then we smoked it for

> approximately three to four days in the smokehouses until it was finished. I used apple and hickory wood to hand fire it. We had two smokehouses; they each held about 6,000 pounds. They were the old wooden smokehouses, we hung them three tiers high.[3]

Several bologna makers claim one of the key factors that can affect the taste of the bologna is the smoke and the wood used to create that smoke. The Palmyra Bologna Company uses 10 wooden smokehouses that can hold up to 16,000 pounds of product, according to Ron Fouche, the company's quality assurance manager. The company uses only hard woods, such as hickory, to smoke the meats.

Landuyt said Weaver's uses smokehouses in a different way.

> We put smoke in a product, but by using a starter culture we were able to accelerate the product, instead of hanging in the houses four, five or six days outside, you could actually get it done in 24 hours in another house. And yet you use natural wood, so you had natural smoke but it just didn't take as long to do it.[4]

The bologna can be made in newer stainless steel facilities, which are cleaner, according to Landuyt.

> You control the smoke, you control the air that's going in them and you're not going outside with the elements that the outside has.[5]

Seltzer's Lebanon Bolognas hang inside a smokehouse at the Palmyra plant. Bolognas are smoked over a fire pit covered with sawdust from hardwoods, like hickey or apple, which give the meat its smoky flavor. (Chris Sholly)

As a result of using the newer methods, the need for the old wooden smokehouses has diminished. The wooden smokehouses at Daniel Weaver's plant in Weavertown have been dismantled, although the company keeps a few for other uses.

Eugene Ditzler, a custom butcher who has a shop in Lickdale, Pennsylvania, uses the newer, quicker methods to produce his bologna, but he still uses sawdust to create the smoke to cure the meat.[6] Ditzler confirmed that the difference in flavor between the bologna brands comes from the type of wood that is used in the process. In addition to hickory, other woods used are apple, oak, cherry, maple, and sassafras.[7]

Early types of smokehouses were built of different materials, mostly of wood, but there were also ones that were made of stone, or a combination of stone and brick.[8] The rectangular smokehouses, each about six to eight feet in height and width, contained no windows, the only openings being a door and vents where the smoke would pass out.[9] In the center of the smokehouse was a fire pit or small stone or brick fireplace two to three feet deep.

Before refrigeration was invented, Pennsylvania German farmers would butcher their animals when temperatures were between 30 and 40 degrees because the meat had to be sufficiently cooled, but not frozen, to properly prepare it for the curing process.[10] The meat was cooled for several days before the curing ingredients were added. The smokehouse fire and temperatures had to be kept even; the meat could not be overheated, or it would become soft and not retain the smoked flavor. To make the fire smolder, farmers used heavier materials, such as wood chips or sawdust.[11] The bologna was hung in the smokehouse in muslin or cheese cloth, burlap or cellulose. Ditzler said his family used to buy large amounts of muslin, which they would cut and sew to fit the oblongs. Because that became time-consuming, Ditzler's family switched to plastic bags, which also hold the moisture better, he explained.

Butcher Roy Burkholder believes the key to a good Lebanon Bologna is the bacteria. Bologna-making was almost an art before starter culture was developed, because many factors could affect the process, as he explained:

> Your bacteria were very important in Lebanon Bologna. Usually, we added two pounds of dextrose to one pack of starter culture and it was good for 100 pound of meat. I'd say today you could probably make a much more uniform product than we could back at that time (1960s and 1970s) because back then you had to contend with the weather. There were a lot of things you had to contend with. It made a difference. You got a night that was really windy, whipped up the draft, you had to fight the fire to keep it cool, you know. I would have to get up two hours every night to check that smoke fire. You learned eventually what you needed to do, but there were a lot of factors.[12]

Although Lebanon Bologna is mostly produced in factories today, some farmers and custom butchers make the bologna on a smaller scale for themselves or for local customers. They may or may not use more modern methods, such as the stainless steel ovens that have replaced the old-fashioned wooden smokehouses of the past. Ditzler produces his own Lebanon Bologna using methods he learned from his grandparents, but he has replaced the wooden smokehouses with a more modern oven. Ditzler started making Lebanon Sweet Bologna when he was 18 years old in 1962.[13] His grandparents, who owned a small farm in Lebanon County, were descendants of the early Pennsylvania German settlers and carried on the traditions that were handed down from generation to generation, he said. Among those traditions was butchering cows and pigs in the winter months and making sausages.

Ditzler said Lebanon Bologna can be made from deer meat, as well as from cows and bulls. During deer season, he makes the bologna from venison that hunters bring to him. This bologna is much like the bologna he makes from cows.

Burkholder said his brother, Clarence, who runs a custom meat business called BurPak Inc., near Myerstown, Pennsylvania, processes about 900 deer annually. From that number of deer, he can produce about 30,000 pounds of a bologna a year.[14] But Burkholder believes the deer meat does not make as good a Lebanon Bologna as bull or cow meat:

> If you get your meat fresh and do it right away, it's OK. But if you let you meat lay around too long, because of the way (the deer) was shot and the stress it's under when it's chased, the (meat) doesn't last long. Once when you had a good piece of beef, deer meat doesn't taste so good to you. That's the butcher in me.[15]

Early bologna manufacturers learned through trial and error how to make a tasty Lebanon Bologna. Weather conditions played a key role in the process. Butchers, such as Burkholder, used their experience and intuition to make good bologna. It has been only in the past three decades that modern manufacturers have learned more about the actual chemical processes that takes place in the curing of the meat and have used that information to develop quicker ways to produce bologna. Whether these new developments make a better Lebanon Bologna than the old-fashioned wooden smokehouses is open to debate.

This is an example of the smokehouses that were once used for making Lebanon Bologna at Daniel Weaver's company in Weavertown. At one time, this particular smokehouse was used as a retail outlet where customers could purchase products. The smokehouse is no longer used, except as a display. (Chris Sholly)

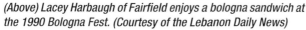

(Above) Lacey Harbaugh of Fairfield enjoys a bologna sandwich at the 1990 Bologna Fest. (Courtesy of the Lebanon Daily News)

(Right) Ester Yeakley of Myerstown fries Kutztown Bologna on a grill at the Bologna Fest in 1990. The festival was one of the ways in which local people celebrated the favorite Pennsylvania Dutch meat in the early 1990s. The festival drew hundreds of tourists, but it was cancelled after a few years because of waning attendance. (Courtesy of the Lebanon Daily News)

Most Pennsylvanians are familiar with Lebanon Bologna. It's a unique product that has been part of the foodways of the state, in particular in central Pennsylvania, for more than 100 years. Because it is special, many people often send the bologna as a gift to relatives and friends. Brian Weaver said his Little Dutch brand has been sent to soldiers serving overseas since World War II:

> We sent Lebanon Bologna overseas during all the wars. A soldier at the U.S. Embassy in Moscow one time during the Cold War got a (bologna) sandwich from one of our (U.S.) sergeants. The sergeant said it was the first time he ever heard a Russian admit that we make something better than they do.[1]

Many Lebanon Countians who move to other states always look forward to getting a package of Lebanon Bologna from home, or they buy some to take with them when they come back to visit. Lebanon County Judge Robert J. Eby remembered eating Lebanon Bologna "all the time" in college:

> When I went to law school, I lived with three other guys and I would make fried bologna sandwiches and such. They thought it made the apartment and the refrigerator smell so bad, they wanted me to get my own refrigerator to keep the bologna in.[2]

People associate the distinctive taste of Lebanon Bologna with the Pennsylvania Dutch region. But it's not a taste that appeals to everyone. Butcher Roy Burkholder said:

The Lebanon County tourist bureau started the annual Bologna Fest to attract more visitors to the area and to celebrate the bologna-making industry that helped make the county famous. This is one of the early brochures featuring scenes from the 1985 event. (Courtesy of the Lebanon Daily News)

> "It's a taste that either you like or you don't like. It's something that people are raised with and they're used to having it. Take it out of this area and people don't like it."[3]

Brian Weaver agreed:

> Outside of central Pennsylvania they just don't know what it is. Some people think 'What do I do with it? Do I cook it?' Because it's a redder-type meat, people have no idea what to do with it.[4]

But for those who grew up with the taste, Lebanon Bologna has come to symbolize home and tradition. The physical characteristics of the sausage—its aroma, appearance, taste, branding—remind those who grew up in Central Pennsylvania of their roots.

The German farmers who first developed the bologna in the early 1700s settled in a land that was still a frontier. They worked hard to cultivate the land and to survive off of what they grew and made. By nature, they were a very thrifty people, who could little afford to waste anything. Meat was an essential, life-sustaining food. Four to six ounces of meat contains 100 percent of the daily protein an adult needs.[5] So, meat could not be

The Bologna Fest featured many activities, such as bologna throws, entertainment, carnival rides, and plenty of Lebanon Bologna, as well as other foods to eat. (Courtesy of the Lebanon Daily News)

wasted, and German farmers adapted the sausage-making techniques they brought from Europe in order to make a new summer-type sausage using the leftover cuts of meat from butchered cows and bulls.

The butchering and curing of the summer sausage that would become known as Lebanon Bologna was a common and well-known practice that some entrepreneurs decided to try in the marketplace. Its unique characteristics made Lebanon Bologna a practical product to market to the growing urban population, thousands of them German immigrants looking for work in the new factories being built as the American Industrial Revolution spread throughout Lebanon County. Like many regions across the United States, there was a high demand for more workers. And these workers needed, and craved, meat. Nationally, beef had become a more affordable, and prized, choice of meat.

As Lebanon Bologna's reputation began to spread from Pennsylvania to other states, the manufacturers began to expand their products to a national market. Newspaper and magazine articles, as well as Pennsylvania natives who moved to other states, also helped to spread this local folk food, so that it has become a product that can be found in many supermarkets around the nation. Indeed, in the 1920s the federal government gave the folk food a permanent place on its list of meats by making it a generic term, like Genoa

Under the careful supervision of the Daniel Weaver Company director of operations, workers gently lowered a 200-pound Lebanon Bologna with the Kutztown label unto a specially made bed where it rested for two weeks in the smokehouse. When it was ready, the bologna was hoisted by a crane and lowered at Citizens Walk Park in Lebanon on New Year's Eve 2006. This is an annual event started in the 1990s, and it is the only real food in the United States lowered for the occasion. (Courtesy of the Lebanon Daily News)

salami, and prescribing what the specific contents of the meat must be in order for manufacturers to label it as "Lebanon Bologna." It was listed as one of the main meats on the nation's rationing list during World War II.[6]

National advertisements for Weaver's and Seltzer's brands of bologna appear in The New York Times in the 1940s. Palmyra Bologna Company quality assurance manager Ron Foućhe recalled that the company shipped Lebanon Bologna by train to customers in Illinois and Indiana when he first started working there in the mid-1950s. He said those customers were primarily Amish and Mennonite families who had moved from Pennsylvania and started groups in those states. Another example of its national reputation can be seen in a 1953 article written by Jane Nickerson, who mentions Lebanon Bologna as a cold cut for warm weather:

> In casting about for candidates for the warm-weather cold cut platter, one will find among the most interesting Lebanon Bologna which the Pennsylvania Dutch originated many years ago. This has a unique and delicious tanginess that derives from the "starter" or "mother culture"; with which the raw beef is combined.[7]

In 1948, another New York Times column mentions a scarcity of Lebanon bologna in New York City. New York City's famous department stores of Macy's and Bloomingdale's once carried the bologna from Pennsylvania, which was considered a specialty product. It sold for about 94 cents a pound then.[8] In company advertisements in the New York Times, it was billed as a Pennsylvania Dutch delicacy or treat, something that had a flavor the reader in New York had never before tasted.[9] By the 1950s, the companies had started selling their products through the mail, sending their products around the world. Lebanon Bologna has survived commercially partly because the companies advertised their brands of the meat. Pennsylvania natives who moved to other places also remained loyal to the meat—even to individual brands—ordering it themselves or receiving it as a gift from family and friends who wanted to give them a little taste of home.

Since 1996, Lebanon Bologna has served as a symbol of the community in another

A crowd gathers around a 200-pound Lebanon Bologna in downtown Lebanon as it is lowered to ring in the New Year on Dec. 31, 2007. The annual event draws hundreds of people who are willing to brave rain or snow to see the bologna drop. The bologna in this photo was made by Kutztown Bologna Company of Lebanon County. (Courtesy of the Lebanon Daily News)

way. A bologna is dropped on New Year's Eve in Citizens Walk at Ninth and Cumberland Streets, close to the Lebanon Farmers Market in Lebanon, to bring in the New Year. Dropping an object of local significance from a building on New Year's Eve is an event that is becoming popular in many communities around the region and the United States. These objects usually represent the community's identity in some way. Unlike other symbols dropped on New Year's Eve, the Lebanon Bologna that is used is a real food, not a papier-mâché replica, and according to organizers of the event, the only edible object dropped anywhere in the United States on that night. After being dropped, the bologna is sliced into appropriate sizes and donated to a local homeless shelter. Jody Kasperowicz, a representative of the Community of Lebanon Association who originated the event in 1996, said the group wanted to drop something distinctive and related to the Lebanon area:

> At the time, Betty Eiceman was Mayor, and she was very receptive to the idea. We had great cooperation from the city. At that time we did a parade to lower it (a bologna). The city worked well with the Community of Lebanon Association bringing it all together. I think people associate it with our area. I think [it triggers] a lot of tradition and memories. I guess because of the name that carries through with the piece of meat.[10]

Kasperowicz said she has been interviewed by radio station personalities in Florida, Mississippi, and Arkansas, who were intrigued by the idea of a bologna drop. "One of the radio stations wanted me to sing the bologna song from Oscar Meyer. You know, 'My bologna has a first name.' I told them no, this isn't Oscar Meyer. This is a totally different breed of bologna."[11] The New Year's Eve drop draws several hundred people, regardless of the weather, to the watch city firemen lower the Kutztown-brand bologna, which is donated by Jerry Landuyt. The size of the bologna is usually an 11-foot-long, 200-pound log of meat.

In the 1980s, the community celebrated the home-grown bologna with a festival. The Lebanon County tourism bureau originated the annual Bologna Fest. For several years the event was very popular, attracting about 20,000 visitors. The festival featured a variety of activities and there was plenty of Lebanon Bologna to consume, including one bologna that was more than 60 feet long and weighed 1,202 pounds.[12] Festival expenses,

WANTED

A Bologna Queen

AGE: Contestants must be between the ages of 17-23 at the time of the contest — August 26, 1988. You must be single, never married, and agree to remain single during your reign if selected.

APPEARANCE: You will be judged on poise, appearance, personality, style, intelligence, speaking ability, enthusiasm for Lebanon County and general wholesomeness.

PRIZES: The honor of representing Lebanon County's major industry, plus $100 dollars cash, $100 worth of Mary Kay Cosmetics, a $700 wardrobe, and an annual opportunity to receive appearance fees.

APPLICATIONS: For complete details and an application, send your name and address to "Queen Committee", Lebanon Valley Tourist Bureau, Quality Inn, P.O. Box 626, Lebanon, PA 17042.

however, began to outstrip revenues, and it was last held in 1997.[13]

Lebanon has come to identify itself with the bologna. The community's pride in the product can easily be seen in the way it is shared with visitors and in the enthusiasm for the New Year's Eve drop. Although it was commercialized, Lebanon Bologna is still a traditional product, being made essentially the same way German settlers first made it. Generations of local residents have grown up with its distinctive flavor and texture, and people will most likely continue to enjoy it in the future. And, as the Pennsylvania Dutch saying goes, "That ain't no baloney" —at least, it's no _ordinary_ bologna.

For the 100th anniversary of the Daniel Weaver Company, a decanter was made in the shape of a smokehouse with Weaver's Lebanon Bolognas smoking inside. The decanter was made by the Michter's Distillery for the occasion. The Lebanon County Historical Society has one of the decanters. (Lebanon County Historical Society)

The Bologna Man was the creation of Mark Buffamoyer, a Bethel Township resident. The costumed character appeared at the Bologna Fest and other local events but was not endorsed as the "official" symbol of any event. (Courtesy of the Lebanon Daily News)

Notes

Chapter I

1. Mehler, Genevieve. Personal interview. 6 February 2007.
2. "Business Directory of Lebanon County, Pa.1868-69." Grittinger, Seltzer & Light. Sherman & Co. Philadelphia, page 24.
3. May, George. Palatine and Scot-Irish Settlers, Lebanon County Historical Society, Vol. 1 No. 15, page 305.
4. ibid, 308.
5. Yoder, Don. "The Sausage Culture of the Pennsylvania Germans." Food in Perspective: Proceedings of the Third International Conference on Ethnological Food Research. Eds. Alexander Fenton, Trevor M. Owen, Edinburgh: Donald, 1981, page 411.
6. ibid, 412.
7. ibid, 410.
8. ibid, 412.
9. ibid, 411-412.
10. ibid, 411.
11. Wheeler, Mary Greiner, Personal interview. 26 September 2006.
12. Burkholder, Roy. Personal interview. 2 February 2007.
13. ibid.
14. ibid.
15. Shapiro, Stephanie. "Taste: A Slice of History." The Baltimore Sun. 9 November 2005. Section F, page 1.
16. Yoder, 413-414.
17. ibid, 414.
18. ibid, 415.
19. Weaver, William Woys. Sauerkraut Yankees: Pennsylvania Dutch Foods and Foodways: Harrisburg: Stackpole Books, 2002, page 40.
20. Wheeler, 2006.
21. ibid.

Chapter II

1. Boyd, William H. "Boyd's Lebanon Directory: 1883-84." Pottsville, Pa., page 13.
2. "Bolognas." Local Affairs. Lebanon Courier. 21 March 1872, page 3.
3. Weddle, Harry Jr., Personal interview. 17 November 2006.
4. "Geo. T. Brooks, Butcher." Lebanon Courier. 15 April 1873, page 1.
5. Ferris Bros. "Lebanon City and County Directory: 1887-88." Philadelphia, Pa., page 193A.
6. "Lebanon Famed for Bologna." Evening Report. 10 September 1912, page 9.
7. "George T. Brooks Died Sunday: Ill Only Short Time." The Evening Report. 3 January, 1921, page 3.
8. ibid.

9. "Lebanon's Great Bologna Industry." Lebanon Daily News. 7 June 1911, page 3.

10. "Butcher Geo. Brooks Leaves for Chicago." Lebanon Daily News. 1 January 1913, page 1.

11. "Morris Packing Co. To Manufacture Famous Lebanon Bologna Here." Lebanon Courier. 6 March 1916, page 1.

12. "Lebanon's Great Bologna Industry."

13. ibid. The company is sometimes referred to as E.L. Brooks. I believe the initials refer to Brooks' youngest daughter, E. Laura. Pennsylvania Corporation Bureau documents, however, list the name simply as Brooks Bologna Company.

14. "And Butcher Brooks Still Makes Bolognas." Lebanon Daily News. 22 February 1913, page 3.

15. "George T. Brooks Died Sunday: Ill Only Short Time."

16. Pennsylvania Department of State. Corporations. Business Entity Filing History. Brooks Bologna Company. Entity No. 46088. Date: 1 January 1926. Creation Filing: Microfilm No. 2880, Start 62. Date: 25 July 1938. Amendment: Microfilm No. 7520, Start 63.

17. "Swift And Co. Plant Sold To Palmyra Firm." Lebanon Daily News. 18 July 1970, page 1. In Lebanon County, Pa., Recorder of Deeds Office in deed book 8-COR-85 is a transaction between Swift & Company and Mary E.B. White on October 14, 1936. Records filed with the Pennsylvania Department of State Corporation Bureau show company officials Vice President L.O. Alkire and Treasurer J. Bliss filed an application to dissolve Brooks Bologna Company on July 25, 1938. In addition to Alkire and Bliss, the officers of the company were listed as A. L. Tolin, president and J.E. Corby, secretary. Of those, Tolin's address was listed as Seventh and North streets in Harrisburg, and the rest were listed as Stock Yards Station, Chicago, Ill. Other Directors of the Board were A.A. Johnston, who had the same address as Tolin and D.W. Creeden of Chicago.

18. Weddle, Harry Jr., Personal interview. 17 November 2006.

19. "Lebanon Famed for Bologna."

20. "Death Summoned Former Mayor Conrad G. Gerhart Early Sunday Morning." Lebanon Daily News. 1 February 1926, page 1.

21. "Death Claims Former Mayor C. G. Gerhart: Octogenarian Banker and Successful Business Man Ends Long Career. Civil War Veteran." The Evening Report. 1 February 1926, page 1. Also, Beers, J.W. & Co. Biographical Annals of Lebanon County, Pa., Chicago, 1904, Conrad Gerhart, pages 120-122.

22. "Death Claims Former Mayor C. G. Gerhart: Octogenarian Banker and Successful Business Man Ends Long Career. Civil War Veteran." The Evening Report. 1 February 1926, page 1.

23. "2,500 Pounds of Bologna." Lebanon Daily News. 6 January 1892, page 1.

24. "Manufacture of Bolognas." Lebanon Daily News. 2 February 1892, page 1.

25. "Death Summoned Former Mayor Conrad G. Gerhart Early Sunday Morning." <u>Lebanon Daily News</u>. 1 February 1926, page 10.
26. ibid.
27. Beers, J.W. & Co. <u>Biographical Annals of Lebanon County, Pa.</u>, Chicago, 1904. Daniel Weaver, page 167-168.
28. Ibid, 166.
29. ibid, 166.
30. "Sudden Death Daniel Weaver in Florida." <u>Lebanon Daily News</u>. 24 May 1926, page 1.
31. Heilman, 13.
32. "Received its Charter." <u>Lebanon Courier</u>. 31 January 1906, page 2.
33. Ibid. The directors' shares were: Weaver, 2,660; Brooks, 320; Eby, 1,320; Seeger, 660; Herr, 1,330; Kreider, 410; and Bomberger, 135. The other shareholders and the number of shares were: John S. Weaver of Prescott, 85; John H. Steiner of Prescott, 85; Ray T. Sherman of Lancaster, 1,330; Edward Seeger of Lebanon, 660; G. Irwin Ranck of York, 270; Walter Loose of Reading, 270; Isaac B. Krall of Reistville, 135; Joseph G. Kelchner, 190; and Abraham H. Burkholder of Palmyra, 140.
34. "Realty Transfer: Mr. Weaver Transfers Some Holdings to his Son." <u>Lebanon Courier</u>. 13 April 1909, page 2.
35. Sudden Death, page 1.
36. ibid.
37. Verlaque, Laura. Pasadena Museum of History. Personal e-mail. 25 January 2007.
38. Neff, Daniel W. Personal interview. 24 January 2007.
39. Sudden Death, page 1.
40. ibid.
41. ibid.
42. "Arrived Here from Mexico: Ray Sherman is engaged in Bologna Business. Owing to Insurrection business is at a standstill-No damage to his property." <u>Lebanon Daily News</u>. 18 April 1911, page 1.
43. Martinez, Oscar J. <u>Border Boom Town: Ciudad Juárez since 1848.</u> Austin & London. University of Texas Press, 1975, page 19.
44. ibid.
45. Pilcher, Jeffrey M. <u>The Sausage Rebellion: Public Health, Private Enterprise, and Meat in Mexico City, 1890-1917</u>. Albuquerque. University of New Mexico Press, 2006, page 6.
46. Martinez, page 42.
47. Seltzer, H. Jack. Letter to the author. 7 February 2007.
48. Leffler, Sara Greiner. "It's Bologna." Dauphin County Historical Society, Harrisburg, Pa. 17 October 1955, page 4.
49. "John Weaver and His Wife to Visit Mexico: Will Look Over His Large Cattle Ranch and Bologna Factory Confiscated by Villa." <u>Lebanon Courier.</u> 31 January 1919, page 4.

50. ibid.
51. Greiner, Eleanor L. Personal interview. 20 April 2007.
52. "Left on Tuesday for Mexico Home." Lebanon Courier. 1 January 1913, page 1, and "Lebanonians Return Home From Mexico." 24 March 1919, page 1.
53. "Mexicans on Warpath: Local Bologna Firm Interested in the Insurrection Down South." Lebanon Courier. 12 February 1912, page 1.
54. "John S. Weaver Fatally Injured: Prominent Local Citizen Is Tossed From His Buggy." Lebanon Daily News. 2 August 1943, page 1.
55. Leffler, page 4.
56. Hower, Elsie. Personal interview. 17 November 2006.
57. Weaver, Brian. Personal interview. 13 February 2007.
58. ibid.
59. ibid.
60. "Robt. L. Eby—Wholesale Grocer." The Evening Report. 11 September 1912, page 8.
61. ibid.
62. Eby, Robert J. Eby. Personal interview. 23 January 2006.
63. Bachman, David. Personal interview. 5 February 2007.
64. "Cry of Fire Stirs Many: Robert L. Eby's Bologna Plant Breaks Out in Flames." Lebanon Daily News. 28 March 1913, page 3.
65. ibid.
66. Horowitz, Roger. Putting Meat on the American Table: Taste, Technology, Transformation. Baltimore. The Johns Hopkins University Press, 2006, page 19.
67. ibid, page 19.
68. ibid, page 28.
69. Seltzer, H. Jack Letter to the author. 7 February 2007.
70. Horowitz, page 30.
71. Pennsylvania Department of State. Corporations. Business Entity Filing History. Eby Bologna Company. Entity No. 105179. Date: 1 January 1915. Creation Filing: Microfilm No. 2390, Start 116.
72. "Morris Packing Co. To Manufacture Famous Lebanon Bologna Here." Lebanon Courier. 6 March 1916, page 1.
73. Lebanon County, Pa., Recorder of Deeds Office. Deed Book, Vol. COR 2, page 776.
74. "Eby Bologna Co. Buys Seeger Plant: The Structure will be equipped for a modern bologna plant: To be electrically equipped." Lebanon Courier. 19 October 1917, page 1.
75. "Capital of the Eby Bologna Co. Increased." Lebanon Daily News. 20 March 1918, page 1.
76. Pennsylvania Department of State. Corporations. Business Entity Filing History. Lebanon Bologna and Provision Company. Date: 1 January 1920. Business Entity Filing History. Entity No. 201133: Microfilm No. 6240, Start 187.

77. Kessler, Robert Sr. Phone Interview. 17 July 2008.

78. Eby, Robert J. Eby. Personal interview. 23 January 2006.

79. Sanborn Map Co. "Insurance Map of Lebanon, Lebanon County, Pa. New York. 1925. New Index, March 1950., page 13.

80. Seltzer, H. Jack Letter to the author. 7 February 2007.

81. ibid.

82. Foućhe, Ronald E. Personal interview. 10 March 2006, 19 April 2006.

83. Seltzer.

84. ibid.

85. "Palmyra Folk to Make California Their Home." Lebanon Courier. 15 March 1912, page 2.

86. "Harvey Seltzer Will Enlarge Bologna Plant." <u>Lebanon Daily News</u>. 5 September 1912, page 1

87. Seltzer.

88. Foućhe.

89. Gallery of Speakers' Portraits, Pennsylvania House of Representatives, <http://www.legis.state.pa.us/WU01/VC/visitor_info/gallery/ SpeakersPortraits.pdf>, H. Jack Seltzer, 29.

90. Reed, Charles A. <u>Men Who Made Palmyra: A Story Told by Dutchman, A Storyteller</u>. Self-published: 2006.

91. Foućhe.

92. ibid.

93. ibid.

94. ibid.

95. "Swift And Co. Plant Sold To Palmyra Firm." <u>Lebanon Daily News</u>. 18 July 1970, page 1.

96. "No salmonella found at Palmyra Bologna Palnt." <u>Lebanon Daily News</u>. 17 October 1995, page 1. The Palmyra Bologna Company recalled 275 tons of bologna in 1995 because the lunch meat was believed to have been the source of contamination. It was found out a week later not to be the case.

97. Baum, Clair, Personal interview. 16 September 2006.

98. ibid.

99. ibid.

100. ibid.

101. Epley, Richard J., Addis, Paul B., Warthesen, Joseph J. "Nitrite in Meat." <http://www.extension.umn.edu/distribution/nutrition/DJ0974.html> University of Minnesota Extension, FS-00974. Revised 1992.

102. Baum.

103. ibid.

104. Zengerle, Mary Louise. "Bomberger Named Agribusiness of the Year." <u>Sunday Pennsylvanian</u>. 3 Feb. 1985: D-1.

105. "County Companies Make Famous Lebanon 'Balony.'" <u>Lebanon Daily News Centennial Edition 1872-1972</u>. 30 September 1972, page F-10.

106. Boyer, Beth. "Seltzer's Bologna to Absorb Bomberger's Lebanon Plant." Lebanon Daily News. 7 July 1987, page 13.
107. "County Companies Make Famous Lebanon 'Balony.'"
108. Burkholder, Roy. Personal interview. 2 February 2007.
109. ibid.
110. ibid.
111. ibid.
112. ibid.
113. ibid.
114. ibid.
115. ibid.
116. Landuyt, Jerry. Personal interview. 18 October 2006.
117. ibid.
118. ibid.
119. ibid.
120. ibid.
121. ibid.
122. ibid.
123. ibid.
124. Shaffer's Directory of the city of Lebanon, Pa. & Suburbs, 1901.
125. R.L. Polk & Co., Lebanon Directory, 1907.
126. "Enter Meat Business." Lebanon Courier. 15 June 1908, page 5.
127. ibid.
128. "A New Bologna Factory." Reading Eagle. 17 June 1908, page 10.
129. "To Sell Seeger Plant." Lebanon Courier. 9 January 1912, page 1.
130. "Seeger Plant Brings $5000 at Sale." Lebanon Courier. 9 September 1913, page 5.
131. Heilman, Robert A. Lebanon Bologna: Its Origins and History. ms A2265-1. Lebanon County Historical Society, Lebanon, Pa., 2000, page 14.
132. "Engine Installed." Annville Journal. 27 January 1906, page 4.
133. "Company Incorporated." Annville Journal. 27 January 1906, page 4.
134. Schaeffer, Blanche M. Personal Interview. 16 June 2008.
135. Heilman, page 14.
136. ibid, page 14.
137. ibid, page 14.
138. "To My Regular & New Patrons." Daniel Weaver Business Card provided by Daniel W. Neff. Personal interview. 24 January 2007.
139. Heilman, page 14.
140. ibid, page 15.

Chapter III

1. Smith, Jason L., Palumbo, Samuel A. "Microbiology of Lebanon Bologna." Applied Microbiology, American Society for Microbiology. October 1973, page 489.

2.   ibid, 489.
3.   Burkholder, Roy. Personal interview. 2 February 2007.
4.   Landuyt, Jerry. Personal interview. 18 October 2006.
5.   ibid.
6.   Ditzler, Eugene F. Personal interview. 8 March 2006.
7.   Long, Amos Jr. The Pennsylvania German Family Farm: A regional Architectural and folk cultural study of an American agricultural community. Breinigsville: The Pennsylvania German Society, 1972, page 189.
8.   ibid, page 179.
9.   ibid, page 179-180.
10. ibid, page 182.
11. ibid, page 188.
12. Burkholder, 2007.
13. Ditzler, 2006.
14. Burkholder, 2007.
15. ibid.

Chapter IV

1.   Weaver, Brian. Personal interview. 13 February 2007.
2.   Eby, Robert J. Eby. Personal interview. 23 January 2006.
3.   Burkholder, Roy. Personal interview. 2 February 2007.
4.   Weaver, Brian, 2007.
5.   Horowitz, Roger. Putting Meat on the American Table: Taste, Technology, Transformation. Baltimore. The Johns Hopkins University Press, 2006, page 3.
6.   "Rationing Point Changes." New York Times. 25 Dec. 1944, page 15.
7.   Nickerson, Jane. "Variety of Cold Cuts for Warm Weather." New York Times. 17 May 1953, sec. Sunday Magazine, page 52.
8.   "News of Food: Pressure Cooker Shaped Like Frying Pan Will Be Placed in the Stores Here." New York Times. 1 Sept. 1948, page 27.
9.   Seltzer's Lebanon Bologna. Advertisement. New York Times. 28 September 1952: sec. Sunday Magazine, page 41.
10. Kasperowicz, Jody. Personal interview. 31 December 2006.
11. Latimer, John. "Bologna star of city's celebration." Lebanon Daily News. 31 December 2006, page 1.
12. Ebeling, Eric. "Plug pulled on annual festival." Lebanon Daily News. 18 July 1997, page 1.
13. Ebeling, Eric. "Holy smokes! Kutztown workers make 100-foot Lebanon bologna." Lebanon Daily News. 1 Aug. 1992, page 1.

Additional references

Levenstein, Harvey A. <u>Revolution at the Table: The Transformation of the American Diet</u>. New York. Oxford University Press, 1988.

Strasser, Susan. <u>Satisfaction Guaranteed: The Making of the American Mass Market.</u> New York. Pantheon Books, 1989.

Camp, Charles. <u>American Foodways: What, When, Why and How We Eat in America.</u> Little Rock: August House, 1989.